FREDERICK BARBAROSSA

Covering one of the most fascinating yet misunderstood periods in history, the MEDIEVAL LIVES series presents medieval people, concepts and events, drawing on political and social history, philosophy, material culture (art, architecture and archaeology) and the history of science. These books are global and wide-ranging in scope, encompassing both Western and non-Western subjects, and span the fifth to the fifteenth centuries, tracing significant developments from the collapse of the Roman Empire onwards.

SERIES EDITOR: Deirdre Jackson

FREDERICK BARBAROSSA

G. A. LOUD

REAKTION BOOKS

To Kate,
And in memory of Alheydis Plassmann (1969–2022)

Published by Reaktion Books Ltd
Unit 32, Waterside
44–48 Wharf Road
London N1 7UX, UK

www.reaktionbooks.co.uk

First published 2025
Copyright © G. A. Loud 2025

Printed and bound in India by Replika Press Pvt. Ltd

A catalogue record for this book is available from the British Library

ISBN 978 1 83639 022 0

CONTENTS

Statue of Frederick I Barbarossa, Imperial Palace of Goslar.

Preface

The American medievalist John Freed began his 2016 biography of Frederick Barbarossa, the most recent book about the medieval emperor written in English, by saying that he had wanted to write a short biography but had soon realized that it would be impossible without totally distorting the historical record. Given this opinion by my distinguished predecessor, it might seem folly, or at least hubris, to try to do precisely that. But admirable as Freed's book is, it weighs in – I use that verb advisedly – at more than six hundred pages. One suspects that only the most determined of professional historians and a handful of unusually dedicated students will ever read it from cover to cover. The most modern full-scale German-language biography is even longer, but the author of that book, Knut Görich, has recently issued a much briefer introductory study for the general reader. I am therefore following his example. I have attempted here to explain not just what happened in the reign of Frederick Barbarossa but why that reign was historically significant, in a way that will be comprehensible to a reader coming fresh to the subject. There are inevitably some omissions and simplifications, especially where there are difficult problems in interpreting the original sources on which there has been no space to dwell, but I have tried to avoid overdue simplification and outright distortion. Although this is (I hope) a work of scholarship, I have dispensed with the full paraphernalia of referencing authorities that would be part of an academic monograph. There *are* endnotes, but apart from in the introduction, I have confined these to where I have quoted, paraphrased or specifically discussed passages in the original sources. Where English translations of these sources are available, I have made reference to these rather than to the original texts in Latin.

Introduction

The reign of Frederick I Barbarossa has often been seen as the high point of the medieval Western, or German, empire – often (anachronistically) known as the Holy Roman Empire. During Frederick's reign (1152–90) this empire was, or so it has been argued, at the height of its power and prestige, before a rapid decline ensued. The premature death of his son Henry VI in 1197 ushered in a period of civil war in Germany. This was followed by the rule of the latter's son, Frederick II (king 1212–50), who was largely an absentee, spending his time in Italy and for the most part leaving Germany to its own devices. Thereafter, an interregnum of almost twenty years when there was no general recognized ruler was followed by the election as king of a minor prince from the extreme south of Germany, Rudolf of Habsburg, in 1273, whose authority was weak and who was never crowned emperor. During the later Middle Ages the nominal rulers of Germany reigned, but rarely actually ruled, other than over their own personal lands. They were no more than 'first among equals' among the German princes, who concentrated upon the development of their own territories, and paid little more than lip service to the supposedly superior authority of the king or emperor.[1] As one shrewd observer, a papal legate and future pope, commented in the mid-fifteenth century, 'you [the German princes] only obey him as far as it pleases you, and it pleases you as little as possible.'[2] Furthermore, as time went on the practice of partible inheritance tended to fragment princely dominions; the so-called 'imperial cities', or at least the larger and more powerful ones, became increasingly independent; and by the eve of the Reformation circa 1500 Germany resembled a patchwork quilt or mosaic of some three hundred different political authorities, a few still powerful in their local sphere, such as the Duchy of Bavaria, but many others minuscule in extent and politically negligible. It was, therefore, hardly surprising that the reign of Barbarossa was seen by later centuries as a 'golden age' of imperial power, when the emperor was still the dominant figure in medieval Christendom, rather than the largely nominal ruler of a divided kingdom.

Frederick Barbarossa had impressed his contemporaries, both as a dynamic ruler and as a personality – insofar as we can separate the individual from often conventional encomia in the sources. His authority, especially in the early years of his reign, appeared strong. His biographer, Rahewin, who continued the *Deeds of Frederick* commenced by the latter's uncle Bishop Otto of Freising, remarked, concerning a diet or court which met in Burgundy in 1157, 'the whole world recognized him as the most powerful and merciful ruler, and undertook, with mingled love and fear, to honour him with new tokens of respect, [and] to extol him with new praises.'[3] A few years later a writer from Bergamo in northern Italy wrote an epic poem in the style of Vergil about Frederick's early campaigns in Italy, to some of which he appears to have been an eyewitness. Frederick himself was portrayed here as a heroic warrior, usually pious and kindly, but terrible too when his anger was (justly) roused: as his modern editor commented, he was to the author 'like a true hero wrestling with other-worldly demonic powers'.[4]

In retrospect, his significance and achievements also seemed clear. He and his grandson Frederick II appeared to be the last two great medieval emperors – and Frederick II, who was born

Statue of Frederick I Barbarossa, Kyffhäuser Monument, Thuringia.

in Italy and spent most of his life there, was less obviously a 'German' figure, as well as, apparently, less successful as a ruler. Nevertheless, a legend developed after the younger Frederick's death in 1250 that he was not really dead but merely asleep in a cave under the Kyffhäuser mountain in Thuringia, ready to wake and restore the empire's glory – and secure social justice within it and reform the Church – when the time was right. Yet by the early sixteenth century this story had begun to attach itself to the figure of Frederick Barbarossa, rather than his grandson, although it took a long time before the confusion was finally resolved and it was generally believed that the sleeping hero must be Barbarossa. During the early nineteenth century this legend, while admitted to being merely a folk tale, was given wider currency by students of folklore like the brothers Grimm, as well as by the poet Friedrich Rückert, whose patriotic poem 'Old Barbarossa', written in 1813, became a widely popular song in a country where nationalist feeling had been stimulated by the Napoleonic Wars. Furthermore, more than half a century later, Barbarossa, viewed as probably the greatest and most successful of the medieval emperors, seemed to be a precursor and role model for the new German 'second empire' created by Bismarck, and ruled (at least nominally) by Wilhelm I of Prussia, after 1871 the emperor of a united Germany. Rückert's poem became indeed a prescribed part of the school curriculum. The connection was made expressly in the paintings commissioned in 1876 to decorate the rebuilt hall of the former imperial palace at Goslar in Saxony, in which Frederick featured prominently, and including a scene where he was shown awaking from his slumbers under the Kyffhäuser. Furthermore, after Wilhelm I's death in 1888, a great equestrian statue was erected in his memory at the Kyffhäuser mountain. At its foot was another sculpture, of Frederick Barbarossa on his throne, with his beard flowing to below his waist, once again waking from his long sleep. The new empire, it suggests, was bringing the great emperor of the past back to life.

Patriotic writers also made the connection by comparing the elderly Wilhelm 1 ('white beard') with his famous predecessor ('red beard'), and equestrian statues of the two were set up alongside each other outside the royal hall at Goslar. Frederick's reign was seen as the high point of the medieval empire, and himself as *the* great emperor, not just by popular writers or nationalist politicians, but even by academic historians. Thus Karl Hampe of the University of Heidelberg, who wrote what became for half a century or more the standard textbook history of Germany in the central Middle Ages, first published in 1909, could describe Frederick's 'heroic personality, the fullest expression of the springtime of German knighthood . . . [He was] strong-willed and active, his hand ever on the sword or the judge's wand.'[5]

The final connection of the medieval ruler with German nationalism and expansionism came in 1941 when the German invasion of Russia was christened Operation Barbarossa – apparently the personal choice of Adolf Hitler. But while one might expect this to have led to an adverse reaction, or at least a loss of interest, in the modern post-1945 democratic Germany, this has not necessarily been the case. Barbarossa and his family (known as the Staufer) may now have been viewed from a less overtly nationalist viewpoint, and more as a cultural and historical phenomenon, but public interest remained strong. An exhibition about 'The Age of the Staufer', sponsored by the state of Baden-Württemberg in 1977, attracted 670,000 visitors in less than three months, and an astonishing 153,000 sets of the massive five-volume exhibition catalogue were sold.

Frederick Barbarossa was king of Italy as well as Germany – indeed possession of the kingdom of (northern) Italy was a *sine qua non* for obtaining the imperial title. While never having the nationalist appeal there that he has had in Germany and being

seen during the Risorgimento as an archetype of the foreign
despot standing in the way of Italian independence, he remains
a figure of some note in modern popular culture. In Umberto
Eco's novel *Baudolino* (2000) the picaresque hero is adopted
by the emperor and tries to make peace between him and the
rebellious Italian cities, before embarking on a search for the
fabled Prester John. Frederick was also the subject, albeit as vil-
lain rather than hero, of an Italian epic film of 2009, with Rutger
Hauer playing the emperor. Here, however, virtue resided with
the Italian cities fighting for their independence, and the real
hero was the (probably mythical) Italian general Alberto da
Giussano of Milan.[6] The political resonance is clear, when one
of the main parties in Italy is called 'the Lombard League', in
direct imitation of the alliance of north Italian cities that opposed
Frederick from 1167 onwards.

While shorn of the anachronistic nationalist undertones
that, at least subconsciously, influenced even such fine earlier
historians as Karl Hampe, the view of the emperor by modern
scholars remains largely positive. Frederick was a great and impressive ruler, not least through sheer longevity, which allowed
him to outlive most of his contemporaries. For example, Karl
Leyser (German by birth but British by adoption, and a brilliant
and original historian) could write that 'Barbarossa was a man
of towering authority. At the end of his reign . . . he stood above
all the other rulers of Europe.'[7] His death as a soldier of Christ,
on his way to retake the holy city of Jerusalem for Christianity,
admired and lamented by contemporaries, and the uncontested
succession of his son King Henry seemed to mark a fitting
conclusion to a turbulent, but outwardly successful, reign. Yet
while not denying Frederick's power and prestige, and his reputation among his contemporaries, perhaps even his charisma,
his reign in reality sowed the seeds for the later decline in the
authority of the medieval emperors. His attempt to restore

imperial rule in northern Italy was a failure; his long quarrel
with Pope Alexander III ended in an embarrassing surrender and
created at the papal court a lasting distrust of him, his dynasty
and overbearing imperial power. Although outwardly his authority as king of Germany remained strong, in fact his reign saw a
haemorrhaging of power towards the princes and the consolida-
tion of their local authority which ultimately replaced effective
monarchical rule. This was, admittedly, a lengthy and evolutionary process. It neither began with Barbarossa's reign, nor was
it finally consolidated until at least the middle of the thirteenth
century. But the reign of Frederick Barbarossa marked an important step along the way, not least because Frederick himself
encouraged this process of devolution. We might debate whether
the change in the balance of political power within the German
Reich was already irreversible by the time of his death in 1190.
Nor can we assume that contemporaries were aware of the long-
term implications of decisions that were made to secure short-
term advantage. But there can be no doubt that the long reign
of Frederick Barbarossa saw far-reaching changes that influenced
the history of Europe for centuries to come. One might also
suggest that, despite his later reputation as a great German hero,
his reign provided an apt illustration of a dictum enunciated
by one of the principal political thinkers of more recent times:
'human beings make their own history, yet they do not make it
as they please in circumstances chosen freely, but [rather] under
the circumstances in which they find themselves, which are
dealt to and inherited by them.'[8]

Let us now, therefore, turn to those circumstances which
shaped the rule of Frederick Barbarossa.

Germany and its principalities in the 12th century.

ONE

Context

By the time of Frederick's accession as king of Germany in 1152 the medieval 'Roman Empire' already had a long history. Charles the Great (Charlemagne), king of the Franks, had been crowned emperor by Pope Leo III on Christmas Day 800. Historians still debate the exact significance of this ceremony and what it may have meant either to the new emperor or to the pope. But the enhanced title was appropriate, both in that by 800 Charlemagne's conquests meant that he ruled over not just one but several different kingdoms and principalities (Francia, Italy, Burgundy, Bavaria, Saxony, Frisia and part of northern Spain), and in that these comprised a very substantial part of what had once been the west of the Roman Empire. Admittedly, this 'empire' failed to last – it was probably too large ever to be effectively ruled by one man or as one polity – and inevitably Charlemagne's heirs disputed over who was to rule which parts of the Frankish empire. At the treaty of Verdun in 843, his grandsons divided the empire into three separate kingdoms. Continued dispute – and the Frankish practice of partible inheritance – led to further fragmentation thereafter. But the memory of Charlemagne, both as emperor and as a great Christian ruler, lived on. For a time the imperial title continued, and indeed for a very brief moment in 887–8 most of the empire was reunited. But the title of emperor became associated with the possession of the kingdom of Italy and rule, at least nominally, over the city of Rome. (In practice the Italian kings were based in the north.) The last Italian king to be crowned emperor was Berengar I of Friuli (whose mother was Charlemagne's granddaughter) in 915. But he was no more than a provincial ruler, who had no authority outside northern Italy and whose hold over even that region was decidedly tenuous. After his death in 924 the Italian kingship was the subject of bitter dispute, and his successors did not seek an imperial title over an empire which no longer existed.

Meanwhile, however, the East Frankish kingdom, the territory of which comprised (roughly) modern Germany west of the river Elbe, Switzerland and Austria, maintained its existence. Its last Carolingian ruler died in 911. The succession devolved, first upon Duke Conrad of Franconia and then in 919 to Duke Henry of Saxony, who added Lotharingia (the Low Countries, the Moselle region and Alsace) to his kingdom. Henry's son Otto, king from 936, overcame several serious rebellions and succeeded in consolidating his rule over his kingdom in a way that his immediate predecessors, who had been little more than first among equals among the several provincial rulers (the dukes), had not. Otto also succeeded in expanding the frontiers of his power base – his own Duchy of Saxony – at the expense of the pagan Slavs east of the Elbe, and in defeating the Magyars, who for half a century had been launching plundering raids deep into Western Europe. The Magyars were also pagan, and in defeating them – and in founding new bishoprics and beginning the evangelization of the Slavs – Otto I and the publicists at his court could portray him as a great Christian ruler and as a worthy successor to Charlemagne. Indeed, Widukind of Corvey, whose *Deeds of the Saxons* was written during Otto's lifetime and dedicated to one of his daughters, alleged that his army acclaimed him as emperor on the evening of his great and decisive victory over the Magyars at Lechfeld, near Augsburg, in August 955.[1]

Furthermore, Otto had already taken over the Italian kingdom in 951, validating his conquest by marrying the widow of the previous ruler, who also possessed her own hereditary claim to the kingdom. So he now ruled over about two-thirds of the old Carolingian empire and was indisputably the most powerful ruler in Christian Europe. The logical corollary to this was his coronation as Roman emperor by Pope John XII in 962. The line of German rulers who succeeded him thus followed in the footsteps of Otto I, not least in that they too sought the imperial title through coronation by the pope at Rome. But their regal status did not in any sense depend on this ceremony, which usually followed several years after their royal inauguration. Thus, for example, Henry II, Otto I's great-nephew, became king in 1002 but was only crowned emperor in Rome in 1014.

Three features of this medieval empire are particularly worthy of note. First, whatever nationalist historians of the nineteenth and twentieth centuries may have said, it was not, at this early stage, 'German'. There was no Germany in the tenth century, and indeed the term 'German' was rarely, if ever, used before the second half of the next century. To Otto I and his contemporaries the East Frankish kingdom was composed of several different peoples from the various duchies of the kingdom: Saxons, Swabians, Franks (Franconians), Bavarians and Lotharingians. Each group had its own laws, and while they could understand each other, each spoke a different dialect. The growth of any sense of German identity was slow. While by the twelfth century the use of 'the kingdom of the Germans' (*regnum teutonicorum* in Latin) was becoming more general, it was still by no means universal. According to Otto of Freising, when Barbarossa addressed the envoys of the people of Rome before his coronation in 1155 he still referred to his own people as 'Franks'.[2] Meanwhile, the classical term *Germania* remained as a geographical expression, not a political description of the kingdom.

Second, far from being 'German', this medieval empire was overtly supranational. Possession of Italy was essential for any claim to be Roman emperor, and in his own eyes at least the monarch was just as much king of Italy as he was of Germany. Between 962 and the death of Otto III in 1002 the emperors spent about a third of their time in Italy, and roughly a third of the surviving documents issued in their name were written for Italian recipients. Admittedly, after that the rulers' visits south of the Alps became less frequent, and usually shorter, but they had no intention of abandoning their rights and powers as king of Italy. It was anyway possible for instructions for the government of Italy to be issued from Germany, and for Italian petitioners to cross the Alps to seek favours and privileges from the monarchs, as the envoys of the city of Lodi did at the beginning of Barbarossa's reign. Furthermore, the emperors at various times also claimed overlordship over other, recently Christianized, kingdoms and principalities along their eastern borders, notably Bohemia, Poland and Hungary, as well as over various Slav principalities between the Elbe and the Baltic coast which were eventually – and largely during the reign of Frederick I – incorporated into the kingdom proper. The Duchy of Bohemia too became more closely a part of the kingdom of the Germans during the twelfth century, albeit a self-governing and distinctive one. Poland and Hungary were more recalcitrant, although the emperors continued on occasion to intervene in their affairs – as Frederick did in Poland in 1157, when the Polish ruler promised him both a monetary tribute and to take part in his forthcoming expedition to Italy, even if in the event he failed to do so. This rule over not just Italy but other lands too was an integral part of the emperors' status. They were not simply rulers over a single kingdom, as other monarchs were. The debate, and it was a long-running and passionate one, among nineteenth-century German historians as to whether the emperor's preoccupation with Italy had 'distorted' the destiny of Germany was therefore anachronistic – telling us far more about political disputes during the age of Bismarck than it does about the attitudes of the Middle Ages.

Third, there was a strong ideological component to imperial rule. On the one hand this was overtly Christian. The emperors were God's representatives on earth, entrusted with the duty of protecting the Church and the Christian people, spreading the faith and, as 'patrician' of Rome, also of protecting and fostering the papacy. To do this, although they were laymen, they possessed numinous, spiritual authority, to safeguard and benefit the Church, and the right to intervene in ecclesiastical concerns. So, for example, Henry II proclaimed in a privilege of 1014 in which he made a monastery subject to the Bishop of Straßburg, 'we have judged that this is in no way contrary to the will of kings, who know how to distinguish the heavenly and earthly domains with a miraculous ordering.' The force of this claim is especially marked, for Henry, who was not just literate but an accomplished Latinist, probably dictated the preamble to this charter to one of the chaplains who staffed his writing office.[3] If the emperors fulfilled these ideals of protecting and favouring the Church then God in turn would protect and favour them. As a diploma of Conrad II explained in 1033, 'our imperial authority is more and more confirmed and strengthened in the kingdom through the grace of God.'[4] Although in this case the document must have been composed by a chaplain or chancellor – for Conrad, unlike his predecessor, was illiterate – we should not assume that therefore he or other rulers would at best have only given lip service to these sentiments, and such texts were no doubt read out to the monarch, in German translation, before they were formally ratified. The inspiration for this Christian rulership was above all Charlemagne, whose canonization in 1166 Frederick Barbarossa attended and probably encouraged, and whom he (or his chancery clerks) praised as 'a model for our conduct and rule' who sought 'to spread the glory of the Christian name and to propagate the worship of the Divine religion'.[5]

Alongside this there was the duty of the ruler to maintain peace and justice, again seen as overtly Christian virtues. Other kings and their advisers would also doubtless have maintained this. But for the emperor there was also the knowledge that he was the successor to the authority of the ancient Roman emperors, the rulers of the known world (or most of it) from the time of Christ onwards. Medieval intellectuals stressed this quite literally: the emperor was the successor not just to Otto the Great or Charlemagne but in direct lineal descent from Augustus and his successors as rulers of ancient Rome. In the religious drama *The Play of Antichrist*, written probably in Bavaria about 1160, it was claimed that 'the whole world was once a Roman fief' and that the current emperor (presumably Frederick was in the author's mind) would restore the glory of the empire to its pristine state.[6] The fullest expression of such views came in the works of Godfrey of Viterbo, an Italian (or possibly of mixed Italian and German ancestry) who spent many years as a chancery clerk writing Frederick's documents before retiring to his native town to write history. Godfrey indeed constructed an elaborate (and almost entirely fictitious) genealogy linking the emperors of the twelfth century with those of ancient Rome, either by direct descent or through marriage connections. Otto of Freising did not go quite that far, but in his *Chronicle or History of the Two Cities*, completed about 1145, he traced the history of the Roman Empire from Augustus onwards down to the then ruler, his own half-brother Conrad III, whom he considered to be the 94th emperor in line from Augustus. And in the speech made by Frederick to the Romans in 1155 that Otto claimed to quote in the *Deeds of Frederick*, he asserted that the virtue and discipline of the ancient Romans had descended to the 'Frankish' emperor. The formal title of the emperors in their own documents during the twelfth century reflected both their God-given authority and this Roman heritage: 'by the favour of divine Clemency, Roman emperor and Augustus'.

Some eighty years before Frederick's accession, however, imperial claims to both spiritual and temporal authority had suffered a severe and damaging challenge. During the 1070s the clerical reformers who had during the previous generation or so gained control of the papal court began to question the validity of imperial authority over the Church. The sins which they alleged were endemic within the ranks of the clergy, above all simony (the purchase of clerical office), were, they claimed, due to laymen owning churches and monarchs and powerful nobles controlling the appointment to bishoprics. The solution was therefore to remove this lay control. And since liberty did not mean license, or absolute freedom, the controlling power that should be substituted in its place was that of papal authority, ultimately justifiable through Christ's commission to St Peter in the Gospel: 'you are Peter and upon this rock I shall build my Church . . . and unto you I have given the keys of the kingdom of Heaven.'[7] Such claims both challenged the ideological authority of the emperor and harmed his ability to govern his realm. Not only did the popes, and especially Gregory VII (1073–85), claim that they as priests and successors to St Peter were superior to any layman, however exalted, and that lay rulers were ultimately accountable to them for their actions, but they were prepared to put this doctrine into practice. In 1076 Gregory excommunicated King Henry IV (who had not yet been crowned emperor) and declared that he was suspended from exercising his kingship. Although the two were subsequently reconciled, with Henry suffering the humiliation of having publicly to beg the pope's forgiveness, this did not resolve the problem. Four years later Pope Gregory once again excommunicated the king, and this time declared that he was irrevocably deposed from his throne. The consequent dispute split western Christendom and lasted for more than forty years (with a brief hiatus between 1106 and 1111), by which time the original protagonists were long since dead.

The quarrel with the papacy was particularly serious for two other reasons. First, German bishops, and some of the richer monasteries, possessed extensive lands and substantial military followings. Often too they had judicial powers within those lands and possessed lucrative rights over tolls and mints – indeed most mints in Germany were located in episcopal cities. The bishops were both wealthy and powerful, and the ruler needed their obedience and cooperation if his authority was to be effective. He and his entourage often stayed in episcopal cities and monasteries as they travelled round the Reich. While the emperors had never controlled every bishopric, especially those on the periphery of the kingdom, during the eleventh century they could in practice probably appoint their own candidates to at least half the sees in Germany, including the six archbishoprics and most of the other wealthy bishoprics. To challenge such authority over the Church was thus damaging to the ruler's secular authority; and apart from any other considerations appointment to a bishopric was the usual reward for his chancellor and chaplains who wrote his documents and 'governed' his empire – insofar as it was directly governed. Furthermore, in Italy the local bishops were the principal agents of imperial rule. But what made the dispute with the Church especially threatening was that at the very same time that it developed, in the early 1070s, Henry IV also faced a major rebellion in Saxony, which was far more widespread, and became far more entrenched than any of the occasional revolts which previous emperors had faced. Had the ruler been facing either one or the other of these challenges he could probably have overcome them: he would most likely have marched on Rome and deposed the obstreperous pope by military force – as indeed some of his predecessors had done. Had he not faced a challenge from within the Church, which some German church-men (though by no means all) came to support, he would almost certainly have overcome the Saxon rebellion – which he came close to doing in 1075, before his excommunication encouraged his opponents to rebel once again. As it was his opponents made common cause against him, and in 1077 the rebels refused to accept Henry's brief reconciliation with the pope and elected a rival king, Duke Rudolf of Swabia.

We need not concern ourselves with the tortuous course of the civil war that raged in Germany for the next twenty years, until a partial settlement in 1098, and which split the clergy of many German bishoprics for a further quarter of a century after that. What was significant was the long-term impact of this extended period of crisis. And what is surprising, at first sight, is that the effects were ultimately more damaging to the emperor's temporal authority than to his control over the Church in Germany, which remained surprisingly strong until the end of the twelfth century. As the dispute with the papacy dragged on, what had begun as a conflict about where supreme authority in Christendom rested became increasingly a much narrower argument as to whether the emperor should have the right to invest new bishops with their episcopal ring and pastoral staff. This ceremony *was* deeply offensive to ecclesiastical reformers since these were the spiritual symbols of the bishop's office, and thus their presentation represented visually imperial claims to oversee the Church in its spiritual as well as temporal aspects. Eventually, after an abortive settlement in 1111 had failed, an agreement was concluded between Henry v and papal legates at Worms in 1122. The emperor agreed to abandon investiture with ring and staff and to allow bishops freely to be elected by their cathedral chapters. But it was also agreed that such elections could take place in the emperor's presence, that if the election was disputed he had the right to intervene to find an appropriate candidate, and that before his consecration the new bishop should receive investiture from the emperor with the temporalities of the see – the lands, regalian rights and secular jurisdiction – which he would confer upon them with his sceptre. The latter was a symbol of secular rule, with no religious connotations, and thus accept-able to the pope and the reform party. But what all this meant was that, despite the promise to allow free elections, in practice the emperor could still exercise considerable influence over who was selected and often impose his own candidates. Cathedral chapters would find it hard to resist a direct instruction from the ruler, made in their presence (or that of a representative delega-tion from the chapter at the imperial court), not least because they hoped for benefactions or privileges from the ruler, and feared his hostility. For example, in 1126 the new king, Lothar III, admittedly on this occasion after consultation with a papal legate, imposed his own candidate as Archbishop of Magdeburg after a disputed election by the canons. His choice was an out-sider from the Rhineland, Norbert of Xanten, the founder of the new order of Premonstratensian canons. (Norbert, a zealous and tactless reformer, proved exceedingly unpopular at Magdeburg and survived several attempts to assassinate him, but he was a loyal follower of the emperor.) So in 1122 the ruler might have surrendered a symbol of his power, but he retained much of its substance.

The rebellion against Henry IV, and the lengthy conflict that it engendered, led to more significant changes. Public author-ity, administered by dukes and counts as agents of the monarch, began to be replaced by the private power of aristocratic families, a small number of whom became increasingly conspicuous. Some of these families had long been important, notably those who became known as the Welfs, in Swabia, and the Babenbergs in the eastern frontier march of Bavaria. Others had more obscure beginnings and would seem to have been, as we would say, upwardly socially mobile. The classic example was the family later known as the Staufer (the name was derived from one of their castles). In 1079 Henry IV replaced his rival for the kingship, Rudolf of Rheinfelden, as Duke of Swabia, appointing in his place a certain Frederick, of whom little is known but who seems to have possessed lands and several castles near Ulm in northern Swabia. To ensure his loyalty, Frederick was then betrothed to the king's daughter, Agnes, despite her being only about seven years old. They were Frederick Barbarossa's grandparents.

The situation that resulted in the Duchy of Swabia encapsulates the process that took place over the entire Reich. Frederick (1) may have been the duke, and the ruler's representative, but he was not unchallenged. The south German allies of the Saxon rebels raised up as rival dukes first the son of Rudolf of Rheinfelden, and after his death in 1090 then another powerful Swabian noble, Berthold of Zähringen, whose lands lay mainly in the Black Forest, in the south of the duchy. (He was married to Rudolf's daughter.) A settlement – we should probably think of it as more of a truce – was only finally reached in 1098. While Frederick was recognized as duke, Berthold was also allowed to retain ducal status – he and his descendants became known as 'dukes of Zähringen'. But while such titles were no doubt important for the prestige and *amour propre* of these noblemen, the reality of power was based not upon them but on more material foundations. The three main dynasties in Swabia, Staufer, Zähringer and Welf, were all striving to increase their possessions and rights, acquire new vassals, develop the economic potential of their lands and consolidate their power in their areas of predominance: the Staufer in the north between Donauwörth and the Rhine, and west of that river in Alsace; the Zähringer in the Black Forest and in what is now Switzerland as far south as Lake Geneva; the Welfs in the east along the

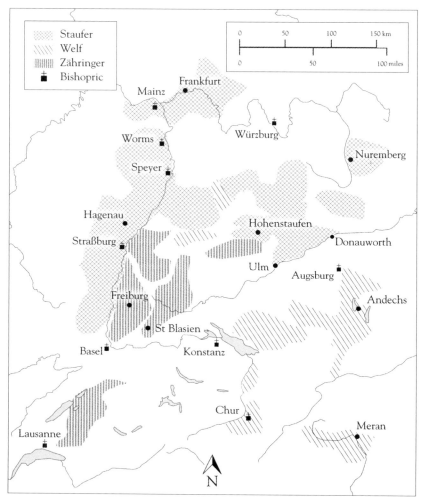

Landholding of princely families in Swabia.

border with Bavaria and as far south as Chur and Meran, deep in the Alps.

They acquired property through marriage connections, from neighbours who died childless or without male heirs, by securing church lands as fiefs (theoretically in return for service), by purchase, or sometimes simply through brute force and intimidation.

They took over or founded mints, gained or levied tolls and acquired comital rights – important because these included judicial powers. They also gained the advocacies of monasteries – the exercise of judicial powers in their lands which abbots, as churchmen, could not exercise directly since these might involve the shedding of blood. They founded towns and markets to boost the prosperity of their lands – and their own income. The Zähringer, for example, founded Freiburg im Breisgau, and the Staufer Hagenau, in Alsace. They built castles to defend their territories and provide bases from which they could be administered. Otto of Freising claimed that Duke Frederick (II) of Swabia, Barbarossa's father, built so many castles that a popular saying developed: 'Duke Frederick always hauls a fortress with him at the tail of his horse,' and that he was so generous with his gifts that 'a great multitude of warriors flocked to him and offered themselves voluntarily for his service.'[8] Such military followings were composed partly of free vassals, knights and noblemen who submitted, or were persuaded to submit, to these aspiring princely dynasties, but many of them were, or became, *ministeriales*. The latter were a class peculiar to Germany, who were both warriors, who would fight as mounted knights, but also unfree, being hereditarily subject to their lords, and could if necessary be transferred to the ownership of another, like other property. But because they were so closely tied to their lords they were inherently reliable (provided they were fairly treated), and they served not only as soldiers but also increasingly as administrators of their lords' lands. Castles and *ministeriales* were the foundations of these burgeoning familial power blocs. But to pay for them lords needed to increase their income – hence the necessity of gaining more land and clearing and cultivating existing territory, the settlers of which would then pay dues to their lords, and gaining fiscal and judicial rights that were financially lucrative.

Such a process was intensely competitive and could often spill over into violence, either directed at weaker neighbours or in feuds with rival families. The crisis of the 1070s may not have begun this competition – the origins are obscure and noblemen were always acquisitive – but it certainly greatly accelerated it. The historian of the Welf family, writing about a century later, described the actions of Welf IV (d. 1101), who was briefly Duke of Bavaria before he fell out with Henry IV, and was restored to that position when they made peace in 1096, but whose family lands were largely in Swabia.

STAUFER GENEALOGY

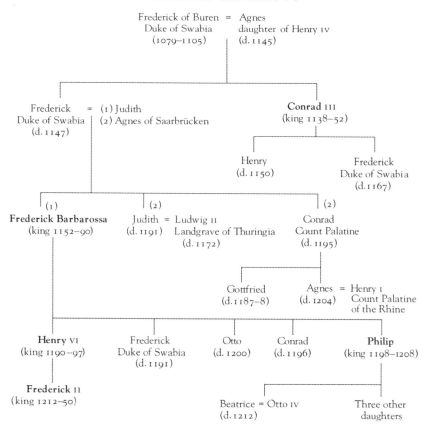

It was he who, first of all our people, because he diminished his wealth inherited from his forefathers by distributing his estates to his supporters in these many violent conflicts, offered his hands to bishops and abbots, and received benefices [fiefs] from them on no small scale. He took possession of all the properties which Count Luithold had in these parts, by donation from him . . . along with the two castles of Acheln and Wulvelingen. He received and obtained the patrimony of Count Otto of Buchhorn, who surrendered this of his own free will during his lifetime.[9]

How much free will was really involved in such transactions is arguable, although Count Otto was childless, which may have influenced his decision.

This growth of territorial lordship (in German *Landesherr-schaft*) led to a fragmentation of authority. Lords enforced their private authority, not that of the Crown. Nor was this process confined to Swabia. Other powerful individuals or dynasties, the ancestors of the later princes, emerged, or consolidated their lands and rule, in different areas of the Reich: notably the Babenberger in southeast Bavaria; the Spanheimer in Carinthia and Istria; and at least three families in eastern Saxony, the Ascanians (counts of Ballenstadt) in the north, and slightly later the Wettins and the Ludowinger (landgraves of Thuringia) along its eastern border. Lothar of Supplinberg, who became emperor in 1125, might well have founded another such nascent princi-pality in east central Saxony had he not died leaving only a daughter – as it was his lands went to his son-in-law, the Welf Henry 'the Proud', which thus gave the Welfs a second power base in the kingdom. And it was not just in Swabia that rival families competed for regional dominance, as for example the counts of Arlon, Brabant and Louvain in lower Lotharingia (in what is now Belgium), all of whom eventually acquired a ducal title. Similarly, in the Moselle valley, also in Lotharingia, during the early twelfth century the archbishops of Trier fought with the counts of Luxemburg and the counts palatine of the Rhine for lands and local predominance.[10]

Contemporaries were in no doubt that this was a period of unusual instability. A contemporary chronicler, Ekkehard of Aura, lamented that even in the 1120s such violence was endemic: 'the storm of civil war and sedition welled up . . . everybody now avenged the injuries done to himself with looting and arson,' and this in turn led to food shortages.[11] While such passages may be

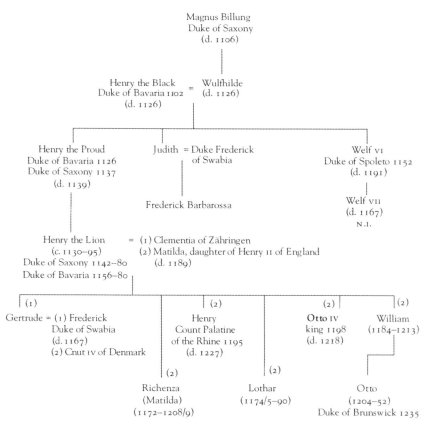

WELFS GENEALOGY

Magnus Billung
Duke of Saxony
(d. 1106)

Henry the Black = Wulfhilde
Duke of Bavaria 1102   (d. 1126)
(d. 1126)

Henry the Proud   Judith = Duke Frederick   Welf VI
Duke of Bavaria 1126   of Swabia   Duke of Spoleto 1152
Duke of Saxony 1137   (d. 1191)
(d. 1139)
                         Frederick Barbarossa   Welf VII
                                                        (d. 1167)
                                                        N.I.

Henry the Lion   = (1) Clementia of Zähringen
(c. 1130–95)   (2) Matilda, daughter of Henry II of England
Duke of Saxony 1142–80   (d. 1189)
Duke of Bavaria 1156–80

(1)   (2)   (2)   (2)
Gertrude = (1) Frederick   Henry   Otto IV   William
Duke of Swabia   Count Palatine   king 1198   (1184–1213)
(d. 1167)   of the Rhine 1195   (d. 1218)
(2) Cnut IV of Denmark   (d. 1227)

(2)   (2)
Richenza   Lothar   Otto
(Matilda)   (1174/5–90)   (1204–52)
(1172–1208/9)   Duke of Brunswick 1235

rhetorical, the violence was very real and even the most important were not immune – Duke Berthold (III) of Zähringen was
murdered in 1122, and ten years later Duke Henry the Proud of
Bavaria was only saved from assassination in an ambush as he
rode unarmed by the selflessness of one of his knights, who flung
the duke from his horse and pretended to be him. And while the
competition between noble families for regional pre-eminence
was the principal motivator, another factor that contributed
to the continuance of instability was the problem of the royal
succession.

Germany from the thirteenth century was an elective monarchy in contrast to most of the other kingdoms of Christian
Europe, where by this period the monarchies were clearly hereditary. But it was by no means inevitable that this would be the
case. The Ottonian dynasty (Henry I and his successors) had seen
three generations of father–son succession, including that of
Otto III, who was only three when his father died. Only when
Henry II died childless and without designating a successor in
1024 was there a genuine election. The successful candidate, a
powerful Rhineland noble called Conrad, was in fact a distant
cousin of the deceased emperor and a direct descendant of
Otto I through one of the latter's daughters. But as king and later
emperor he and his advisers never laid any stress on this relationship – his title derived from his election by his peers, through
whom the will of God had worked. Nevertheless, Conrad was
succeeded in turn by his son, grandson and great-grandson, each
of whom was formally designated as the next ruler and crowned
king during his father's lifetime – Henry IV at the age of three,
succeeding his father, unchallenged, when he was six. So under
the Salian dynasty, as this family became known, the Crown was
once again effectively hereditary. The election of a new monarch
was an acclamation of the sole and obvious hereditary candidate,
not a contest. Admittedly, when the anti-king Rudolf was elected

in 1077, strong exception was expressed to the idea of hereditary kingship; however, this election was carried out by a small group of embittered enemies of Henry IV who were seeking to justify their unprecedented action, and neither Rudolf – who was killed in battle in 1080 – nor his successor as anti-king had much support outside Saxony.

The situation only changed in 1125, when Henry V, like his namesake a century earlier, died childless and without designating a successor. His nephew, Frederick (II) of Swabia, his sister's son, clearly expected to succeed him but this tactless assumption alienated other influential nobles, and the election was anyway stage-managed by one of his personal enemies, Archbishop Adalbert of Mainz. After some rather perfunctory initial discussion, Duke Lothar of Saxony was acclaimed by most of those present. Lothar, it should be noted, had been Henry V's principal opponent within Germany, and Henry's autocratic tendencies had made him far from popular, which probably also worked against the election of his nephew. But had he left a son, a genuine election is unlikely to have occurred. Similarly, Lothar died in December 1137, leaving only a daughter. An election was announced to choose a successor, but, before it could take place, a small group of Staufen supporters hijacked proceedings and announced that they had elected Frederick's younger brother Conrad as the new king and had him crowned at Aachen, the traditional location for such ceremonies. This was therefore a *coup d'état* rather than an election – nevertheless almost all the German nobility concurred and did fealty to him.

In both these cases there was some opposition, and the candidate who had expected to succeed and had failed rose in revolt. Duke Frederick did not put forward a further claim, perhaps because soon after the election he had sworn fealty to Lothar and did not wish to be seen to have committed perjury, but with his support his younger brother Conrad did and indeed was

crowned king of Italy in 1128. He only eventually submitted to
Lothar seven years later. In 1138 Lothar's son-in-law Henry,
Duke of both Saxony and Bavaria, expected to be chosen, had a
fully attended and regular election actually taken place – although
his soubriquet, Henry the Proud, may explain why when he did
revolt there was no great enthusiasm for him, outside Saxony.
Despite his sudden death in October 1139, the disorder continued for several years thereafter because of King Conrad's attempts
to deprive the late duke's son of his father's ducal titles and to
grant these to his own supporters – in the case of Bavaria to his
own half-brother Henry of Babenberg. Henry the Proud's son,
later known as Henry the Lion, still only a child, was eventually
restored as Duke of Saxony in 1142. The fate of the Bavarian
duchy remained an object of dispute in Conrad's last years and
proved to be a major difficulty for Frederick Barbarossa after
his accession to the throne. Furthermore, Welf vi, the younger
brother of Henry the Proud, had rebelled once more in 1149
– it was rumoured after being bribed by the king of Sicily, who
was anxious to prevent a further German expedition to Italy
that might be directed against his kingdom. But, despite this
possible external interference, it was the problems of the royal
succession, created by biological failure to generate male heirs,
that played a major role in causing the breakdown of domestic
peace within Germany after 1125. This was exacerbated by
inter-familial rivalry that spilt over into violence and even
blood feuds. And one of those involved in such disputes was
Frederick, the son of Duke Frederick (ii) of Swabia, the future
king, who was at war with the Bavarian counts of Wolfratshausen
and Dachau in 1146 and then launched a full-scale invasion of
the lands of Conrad of Zähringen. It was probably as part of the
eventual settlement of this dispute that Frederick married Adela,
daughter of Margrave Diepold of Vohburg, who was a relative
of Duke Conrad.

The other significant effect of these problems of authority and law and order in Germany was their impact upon imperial rule in Italy. The dispute with the papacy had already seriously weakened the emperors' position there, for the pro-imperial bishops who were his major supporters were viciously attacked by papal/reformer partisans and sometimes expelled, and their authority over secular matters was much diminished. Furthermore, during the first half of the twelfth century the emperors made only four expeditions south of the Alps. Three of these were directed towards Rome: for the imperial coronations of 1111 and 1133, and Henry v's attempt to install a pro-imperial pope there in 1117–18. Lothar's expedition of 1136–7 was primarily concerned with the new Kingdom of Sicily, the establishment of which was seen as an act of usurpation in territory that should rightfully be subject to the empire. In total during these four expeditions the emperors spent only just over a year in northern Italy, the greater part of which was in Romagna and Tuscany, not in Lombardy. They never, for example, visited Milan, the largest city in the region. Nor, given their concern with matters further south, did they wish to become embroiled in dispute with the northern cities, which too vigorous attempts to assert their authority might well have created. Conrad III, who was busy with internal problems within Germany and then his crusade of 1147–9, never went to Italy during his reign, and was thus not crowned emperor, although he announced his intention to do so, to receive his imperial coronation, shortly before his death in February 1152.

In the emperor's absence, and with the undermining of episcopal authority, a movement for self-government developed among the towns. The leading citizens formed sworn associations ('communes'), who chose their own magistrates and governing councils. The process was a slow and evolutionary one, with considerable hesitation along the way. Generally it was most precocious in Lombardy, and considerably slower in other regions. The first mention of a commune at Milan came in 1117, although it may actually have existed some years earlier since consuls (the principal magistrates) seem to have been in existence from shortly before 1100. By contrast, the first mention of a commune in Florence came only in 1138. But by 1150 most of the larger cities of the north – and especially in the Lombard plain – had been governing themselves for at least a generation and had well-established officials, councils and administrative practices. The largely absentee emperors had so far done nothing to interfere with this process.

By 1152, therefore, the nature of authority in both Germany and Italy had changed considerably, and indeed in the latter kingdom central authority had largely atrophied. The emperor remained a figure of great prestige, but in practice to rule effectively north of the Alps he needed the support of the leading princes and churchmen, and when he went to Italy he would require the cooperation of the northern cities, or failing that their submission to his authority. And while relations between ruler and papacy had been far smoother in the previous quarter of a century than hitherto, there was still an inherent, albeit latent, tension between how the emperor viewed his authority and how the papal Curia did. One advantage that the incoming monarch did, however, possess was that there was a widespread desire within Germany for a peaceful resolution to the various disputes among the leading families that had disturbed the kingdom during the previous reign.

TWO

Early Years, 1152–8

Conrad III died at Bamberg on 15 February 1152. Less than three weeks later, on 4 March, his nephew, Duke Frederick (III) of Swabia, was elected king of Germany at Frankfurt. Five days later, on Sunday 9 March, he was crowned in St Mary's church at Aachen, built by Charlemagne as the chapel of his palace there, the traditional venue for royal coronations. What is striking and unusual about these events is their extraordinary speed. By contrast, Lothar's election in 1125 had followed a full three months after the death of Henry V, not least to give time for as full attendance as possible by the great men of what was a very large kingdom.

The fullest contemporary account of the election came from Frederick's uncle Otto of Freising, who was an eyewitness and one of the bishops who crowned him at Aachen. He stressed the significance of the electoral process: 'this is the very apex of the law of the Roman empire, namely that kings are chosen not by lineal descent, but through election by the princes,' and that Frederick was unanimously elected by 'the entire company of the princes', despite the very short period that had elapsed since the death of Conrad.[1] Yet almost every part of this account may be questioned. First, the electoral principle was by no means firmly established. That there were elections in 1125 and (of a sort) in 1138 was because the deceased emperor had no direct male heir. Conrad III, however, had two sons, the elder of whom,

Henry, was crowned king at the age of ten in 1147, before Conrad departed on crusade. He clearly intended the succession to be hereditary. Henry's elevation during his father's lifetime followed the example of the earlier Salian emperors and was an obvious precaution in case Conrad – already in his fifties – died during his expedition to the Holy Land. However, young Henry had died in the autumn of 1150, aged only thirteen. Perhaps distracted by internal disputes among the princes, Conrad had made no immediate move to replace him by his younger son Frederick, then only five or six. Second, although there were only a few leading men with Conrad when he died, why were almost all the great men of the Reich present at Barbarossa's election less than three weeks later? It seems quite possible that, far from this being simply a wonderful coincidence, as Otto of Freising claimed, they had already been summoned, by Conrad. The obvious reason for this was the designation and election of the latter's son, the younger Frederick, as king, so that he should be established as Conrad's successor before the latter departed on his planned Italian expedition later in the year. That his son was only eight was no bar to his election – in the past other royal sons had been chosen king at even younger ages.

Admittedly, Otto of Freising also said that on his deathbed Conrad had designated Frederick of Swabia as his heir:

> for, being a wise man, he cherished little hope that his son, who was still a small child, would be raised to the rank of king. Therefore he judged it more advantageous both for his family and for the state if his successor were rather to be his brother's son.

Otto also pointed out that Frederick had the advantage that his mother had been a Welf, the sister of Henry the Proud and Welf VI, and that he was therefore well placed to mediate in the family disputes affecting the kingdom.[2] Frederick himself also subsequently claimed, a year afterwards, in a letter to the Byzantine emperor Manuel Komnenos, that Conrad had designated him as his successor.[3] While it is possible that Conrad had had a deathbed change of heart, claims of designation under such circumstances are inherently suspicious. It seems more probable that Frederick took advantage of the king's death, before he could publicly designate his surviving son as his successor, to engineer a coup to seize the throne for himself. He was aided in this by a group of nobles and churchmen who travelled to Frankfurt with him, notably his first cousin Henry the Lion and Bishop Eberhard of Bamberg and the latter's brother Bishop Gunther of Speyer. Henry and Frederick were to be close allies during the early years of his reign, and Bishop Eberhard remained one of his principal advisers until his death in 1170. And an admittedly later chronicle, composed after his death, alleged not only that Frederick deliberately manipulated the election but that he was accompanied by a substantial bodyguard, effectively a small army, with which to overawe the electors.[4] That Frederick was anxious to move as fast as possible to secure his own election also explains why Conrad III was buried at Bamberg, where he died, rather than in the family monastery of Lorch, 150 kilometres (94 mi.) away, where both his father and eldest son had been interred. Escorting his body to Lorch would have wasted precious days. And, once elected, Frederick travelled approximately 320 kilometres (200 mi.) from Frankfurt to Aachen in three days to receive his coronation. There may also, despite subsequent claims as to the unanimity of the election, have been at least one dissenter, for a year later the pope, at Frederick's request, deposed Archbishop Henry of Mainz – who was certainly present and was its nominal host. Was this to punish him for breaking ranks and trying to uphold the claim of the legitimate heir? Hence, far from writing an unbiased description of how Frederick became king, Bishop

Otto was presenting a carefully crafted and sanitized account to disguise a piece of ruthless, if very effective, opportunism.

Frederick was now 29. He had been born, probably, in December 1122. His first public appearance had come when he and his father had witnessed a charter of King Conrad in April 1138, when he was fifteen. This may have marked his formal coming of age. An Italian witness who saw him first when he was in his mid-thirties, and clearly admired him, described him as follows:

> He was of middle height and handsome appearance, having straight and well-made limbs, a white face suffused with red colouration, with blonde and curly hair, and a joyful countenance, so that he seemed always to wish to laugh. He had white teeth and most beautiful hands, and an attractive mouth. He was warlike, slow to wrath, brave and intrepid, active, eloquent, generous but not spendthrift, cautious and shrewd in counsel, of quick mind, overflowing with wisdom, sweet and kind to his friends and good men, but terrible and almost inexorable to evil-doers.[5]

Other sources confirm this description – Rahewin noted also the reddish tinge of his beard[6] – and some of the qualities mentioned, although far from being slow to wrath he seems to have had a quick temper, particularly if he felt that his honour was at stake, although he became better at disguising his feelings as he grew older. A bust, subsequently used as a reliquary, that was commissioned by Frederick's cousin and godfather Otto of Cappenberg, probably to mark his imperial coronation in 1155, may have been a portrait of him, perhaps somewhat idealized, although some scholars consider this to have been simply a generic portrait of a ruler.

Cappenberg bust, c. 1155–60, gilded bronze.

Frederick spoke only German, although over the course of his career he may have acquired some Latin, but he was extremely articulate in his native language – unlike his half-brother Conrad, his father's son by his second marriage, who was noted for his taciturnity. Like most twelfth-century noblemen he was illiterate, but he could depend on a number of highly educated counsellors who could put his wishes into writing, and in Italy legal experts who could formulate his decrees. He could be impetuous and self-willed. He had insisted on joining Conrad's crusade, despite the opposition of his ailing father, who had no wish for his heir to join such a risky undertaking, which would, at best, entail a prolonged absence from Germany. (In fact, Duke Frederick (II) died just before the expedition left.) During the expedition to the east he had punished attacks on his troops in Byzantine territory by burning down a Greek monastery as a reprisal, and during his Italian campaigns he was quite ready to execute as traitors those who were captured fighting against him, although such brutality was contrary to the usual customs of twelfth-century warfare. He could also be stubborn and persistent – qualities that served him well during his military campaigns but could be a handicap politically when he persisted with policies that were clearly not working. And throughout his career he displayed a touchy concern with the reputation and rights of the imperial office (in Latin the *honor imperii*), which often made relations with both the papacy and the Italian cities more problematic than they might have been.

In the months following his accession Frederick had a number of urgent tasks. First, as had become usual, he notified the pope of his election, sending a letter announcing this drafted by Abbot Wibald of Corvey, who had been one of Conrad's principal advisers, and accompanied by a high-ranking embassy, one of whose members was Bishop Eberhard. This was a potentially delicate issue, especially since Frederick did not seek or imply papal

confirmation of his election, as Lothar had done, and probably
also Conrad, but simply notified the pope of what had occurred
as a matter of diplomatic courtesy. Fortunately, Pope Eugenius
was elderly and pacific, and he also needed Frederick's assistance
in Italy, not least in securing control of Rome, whose leading men
were as keen on self-government as those of other cities. His reply
was emollient, welcoming the election. Second, Frederick had
to reward those who had supported him and conciliate potential
dissidents. His clerical supporters like Bishop Eberhard and Abbot
Wibald received generous privileges for their churches – in the
case of these two trusted counsellors only a few days after the coronation. Subsequently, Duke Berthold of Zähringen, whose family
were long-standing rivals to the Staufer, was appointed his viceroy in Burgundy, with wide-ranging powers to act in the king's
absence. (In return he promised to provide troops when the king
should come to Burgundy and for the forthcoming Italian expedition.) Welf vi was granted the title of Duke of Spoleto, which,
although itself conferring no real power upon him, gave him
ducal status alongside the other leading princes and effectively
exempted his lordship in south Germany from the authority of
the dukes of Swabia and Bavaria. Henry the Lion, meanwhile,
was granted the lordship of Winzenburg, whose count had
recently died without heirs, and the lucrative advocacy over the
royal church at Goslar in the Harz mountains, which had valuable silver mines on its lands. Two years later Henry received
the right to establish new bishoprics along the Slav frontier
and to supervise them and their regalian rights as the king did
elsewhere. Perhaps most important, Conrad's son, Frederick of
Rothenburg, despite his tender age, was given the title of Duke
of Swabia and an endowment from the Staufen family lands to
support this. Until his majority his lordship would be under
Frederick's control, but this was a public statement that his
nephew would eventually have an honoured status among the

great men of the new regime and was designed to reassure those
who may have been uncomfortable with Frederick's usurpation
of the throne.

As was customary for new rulers, soon after his coronation
Frederick set off on a progress round his kingdom to show himself as ruler to as many of his subjects as possible and to enforce

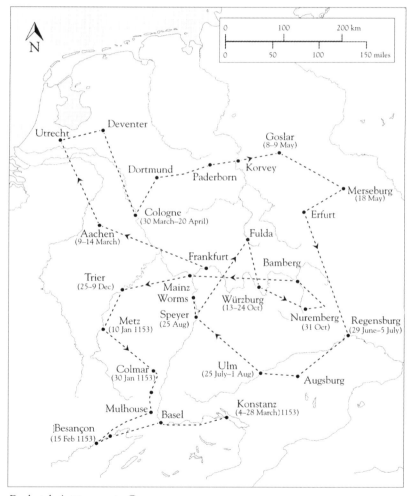

Frederick 1's itinerary in Germany, 1152–3.

his authority by his presence on the ground. Over the first year of his reign he journeyed from Aachen to Utrecht, where he settled a dispute between two rival candidates for the bishopric; then up the Rhine to Cologne, where he celebrated Easter; through southern Saxony to Goslar and Merseburg in May; then south to Regensburg at the end of June, where he met with three archbishops and eight bishops, including Otto of Freising, to discuss the disputed archiepiscopal election at Magdeburg. From there he entered Swabia, reaching Ulm by the end of July, where he issued his first privilege for an Italian recipient, and also a 'land peace' – general regulations for the treatment of malefactors and peacebreakers, including criminal clerics, disputes among knights about fiefs, the carrying of weapons and the safety of travellers.[7] He set off again by a rather circuitous route through Franconia, spending about a fortnight at Würzburg in mid-late October, then via Trier, where he spent Christmas, into Alsace and Burgundy, and finally across through Switzerland (then part of the Duchy of Swabia) to Konstanz, where in March 1153 he met two legates from Pope Eugenius and concluded a treaty with the pope, which was an important precursor to his journey to Italy to receive his imperial coronation. The legates also annulled his marriage to Adela of Vohburg on grounds of consanguinity within the prohibited degrees of kinship – they were both descendants of Emperor Henry III. This was surely at Frederick's own request. There is no evidence that Adela was ever treated as queen, so Frederick may well have already decided to dispense with her before his accession. Why he should have wanted to do so is unknown, although one report, albeit written sixty years later, said that this was because she was notorious for her adulteries. (If true, might this not have occurred while Frederick was absent on the crusade?[8]) But the marriage was also childless, and Adela's relatives were out of favour with the king, so the reasons may equally well have been political.

Frederick, like his predecessors, spent much of his reign on horseback, rarely staying in any one spot for more than a few weeks at most. But while such travelling was the norm, his itinerary during this initial journey round the Reich was unusually extensive and clearly served to cement the authority of a new ruler. Some of the places visited in 1152 only rarely saw him again. It was, for example, to be almost twenty years before he went again to Merseburg, and he seems only to have visited Trier on a further two occasions during his long reign. But, even so, one can note where he did *not* go during his initial tour of the German kingdom. No ruler in generations, apart from Lothar, who was of course a Saxon himself, had travelled to northern Saxony, nor did Frederick at this point – although this was for the most part a thinly populated and undeveloped region. More significantly, although Frederick went to Regensburg he avoided the rest of Bavaria, which is explicable given his tense relations with his uncle Duke Henry, who had been conspicuously absent from his election.

What to do about the Bavarian duchy – or more accurately the ducal title – was the most delicate and difficult issue facing Frederick in his early years as ruler. Henry the Lion had already twice publicly demanded, in 1147 and 1150, that the duchy (which had been held by his father, grandfather and great-grandfather) be restored to him, and now did so again. On the other hand Henry Jasomirgott, as he was known (from his favourite imprecation, 'Yes, so help me God!'⁹) had held the duchy for more than ten years, and had been one of the closest and most loyal allies of his half-brother, Conrad. Frederick's accession had seen, however, significant changes among those who were in favour at court. While Conrad's clerical advisers, such as Wibald of Corvey, continued to serve the new ruler, the lay counsellors were very different. Foremost among those now in favour were Frederick's Welf relations, who had played such an important role in his election. Indeed, Henry the Lion and Welf VI were to witness more of his diplomas during the first ten years of the reign than any other laymen. Frederick probably always intended to restore Henry the Lion to his ancestral duchy, but the problem was how to do this while not permanently alienating Henry Jasomirgott and igniting a feud that might potentially destabilize south Germany and destroy Frederick's efforts to bring peace to the kingdom. Unilateral action to deprive Henry of the duchy might also upset the other princes, who would be afraid of the precedent that this would set. Henry Jasomirgott, meanwhile, did his best to delay any public hearing of the case. He was careful not to defy the king openly and did homage to him at Regensburg in June 1152; and while he ignored several summonses to the royal court he turned up just enough to avoid being considered contumacious. When he did appear, he claimed that there were procedural irregularities that prevented the case being heard. With Frederick anxious to go to Rome and secure his imperial coronation, a decision had to be postponed until he returned to Germany. When Frederick did set off to Italy in October 1154, he was accompanied by Henry the Lion, but the latter's namesake remained at home, still Duke of Bavaria.

Frederick undoubtedly wanted to obtain the imperial crown as soon as was feasible, not least for reasons of prestige, and to avoid delays of the sort that had prevented Conrad III ever receiving his coronation. But the pope was also, for once, anxious that he should come to Rome. In his first letter to Frederick in May 1152, in response to the news of his accession, Eugenius III had reminded him of his uncle's promise to assist the Roman Church (unfulfilled because he had never come to Italy) and asked that Frederick now take over this task. In return, the pope said, he would always strive to increase the king's reputation and fortunes.[10] The pope faced two pressing problems with which he required the future emperor's help. The first was his precarious position in Rome, in the face both of the Roman commune, anxious to rule the city in the papacy's place, and of the incendiary preaching of Arnold of Brescia, a militant reformer who wanted the clergy to observe a strict and ascetic life like the Apostles and denounced the papacy's concern with temporal matters. Second, there was the problem of the Kingdom of Sicily, which concerned both the pope and the new king of Germany.

That kingdom, which comprised not just the island of Sicily but the southern third of the Italian peninsula, had been created in 1130, in the wake of the schism that had occurred after a disputed papal election in February of that year. Anacletus II, the pope who held Rome, had agreed to sanction the royal crown that Roger of Sicily sought, in return for diplomatic and military support. Unfortunately for the new king, Anacletus was the pope who lost the schism. By the time of his death in January 1138, almost all of Christendom, except for the Kingdom of Sicily, had recognized the rival pope, Innocent II, as the legitimate pontiff. And since, in the eyes of the victorious party, Anacletus had never been pope but only a usurper, none of his actions, including the creation of the Kingdom of Sicily, had any validity. Nevertheless, King Roger eventually forced Innocent II to recognize his kingship in July 1139, although to save face the pope issued a bull 'creating' the kingdom, as if for the first time. In theory the king was to be a papal vassal, but in practice relations between him and his nominal papal overlord were often strained. Sicilian troops infringed on papal territory in central Italy, royal control over the Church in the kingdom was considered oppressive and in 1151 Roger had his son crowned co-king without informing the pope, an act of, at the very least, disrespect to his overlord, if not open defiance. Furthermore, many of the cardinals still resented the king's support of the antipope Anacletus and the way in which he had bullied Pope Innocent into confirming his kingdom. And if the Kingdom of Sicily was regarded

as a pariah at Rome, it was even more so in the eyes of the
German ruler, who as king of Italy and successor to the ancient
emperors regarded himself as the overlord over the whole peninsula – even if the kingdom proper was that of northern Italy.
The unilateral creation of the new Kingdom of Sicily was to
German eyes the usurpation of rightfully imperial territory and
authority, and its so-called king a tyrant exercising a rule to which
he had no right. Emperor Lothar had invaded mainland south
Italy in 1137 but any success he had achieved disappeared once
his army withdrew – and he himself died on the way back home.
Conrad was equally hostile and renewed the alliance that his
predecessor had concluded with the Byzantine Empire, directed
against the Kingdom of Sicily. Various south Italian nobles whom
King Roger had exiled also came to his court and encouraged this
policy. But, preoccupied by internal problems in Germany and
by his crusade, Conrad had been unable to devote his attention
to the issue, although King Roger was sufficiently concerned by
the threat of an imperial attack to attempt to stir up trouble
among the German nobles through bribery.

At Konstanz in March 1153 Frederick concluded a formal
treaty of alliance with the papacy. The terms included his promise not to make peace either with the Romans or with Roger of
Sicily (conspicuously *not* accorded the title of king) without the
pope's permission, and to make the Romans subject once more
to the papacy, as they had been in the past. This agreement set
out the agenda for Frederick's first Italian expedition – although
for him the overriding purpose of this journey was to obtain his
imperial coronation. And his determination to impose his and
the pope's authority on the Romans can only have been strengthened by the news, conveyed by the pope to Abbot Wibald, that
a faction in the city had claimed that they had the right to choose
who could receive the imperial crown, as well as by a remarkably
offensive letter sent to Frederick in the autumn of 1152 and

written by an associate of Arnold of Brescia, which not only failed to accord him the royal title but repeated the claim that the 'senate and people' of Rome had the right to elect their ruler and suggested that he send envoys to negotiate about this issue.[11]

The expedition that crossed the Brenner pass into Italy in the autumn of 1154 was quite substantial but not as large as some previous ones, nor the one that Frederick was to lead on his second Italian expedition of 1158. Henry the Lion and Berthold of Zähringen accompanied him, as well as the margraves of Baden and Styria, the archbishops of Cologne and Trier and seven other bishops. Most of these, and apart from Henry the Lion almost all the prominent laymen, were from south Germany. There were only two northern prelates, Gerold of Oldenburg and Anselm of Havelberg. The former had not yet received consecration nor taken possession of his, recently established and very poor, bishopric, and Anselm was a bishop without a see, having effectively abandoned his remote and dangerous diocese on the frontier between Saxony and the (as yet still pagan) Slavs. Neither can have had much, if any, of a following. In all, Frederick had about 1,800 knights, a useful force but not enough really to impose his authority, should he face widespread resistance, although he was joined by two of the most powerful noblemen in northern Italy, Counts Guido of Biandrate and William of Montferrat, both of whom were to be among his most loyal allies in the years to come, who no doubt furnished additional troops.

Frederick did not proceed directly to Rome. He spent six months in Lombardy, from the end of October 1154 until early May 1155, before heading south. In part, this was a matter of 'showing the flag', in a region which had not seen its ruler for almost twenty years. In the first week of December he held an assembly in the plain of Roncaglia, north of Piacenza, to which the various cities sent delegations. Here, at the request of the noblemen of the region, he renewed Emperor Lothar's regulations

about fiefs, promulgated in 1136, the intent of which was to reinforce the position of lords and prevent the alienation of fiefs
without their permission. Frederick also received complaints
from a number of cities about the actions of their neighbours,
notably from Como and Lodi, about the oppression they had
suffered from Milan. At first he seems to have tried to arbitrate
in such disputes and to avoid overtly taking sides – given the
limited size of his army he may have had little option here. Milan,
the subject of most of the complaints, promised the king a substantial monetary tribute and to provide his army with supplies,
and by doing this seemed to have averted any potential hostility.
Yet relations between the largest and most powerful city in
Lombardy and the ruler soon deteriorated. Frederick entered
Milanese territory immediately after the Roncaglia meeting,
whether intending to go to the city itself or perhaps to Monza,
the traditional site for kings of Italy to be crowned, is unclear. But
the promised arrangement for supplies broke down, perhaps unin-
tentionally, and Frederick assumed that this was the result of
malice and blamed the guides the Milanese had provided for
deliberately leading his army into a wasteland. Skirmishes then
broke out between his troops and those of the commune, and a
number of outlying fortresses in Milanese territory were attacked.
While Frederick's army was not strong enough to assault Milan
itself, he decided to make an example of some smaller towns that
he considered to be recalcitrant – although these actions seem
also to have been intended to please his allies. So Asti and Chieri
in Piedmont were destroyed at the request of William of
Montferrat, and in February he laid siege to Tortona, an ally of
Milan, with the encouragement of Pavia – Milan's most important rival in central Lombardy. Tortona put up an unexpectedly
determined defence and only surrendered after a two-month
siege. The inhabitants were allowed to leave unharmed with
their personal possessions, but the town was sacked and then

burned down, with its walls being demolished, or at least badly damaged – an operation into which the Pavians entered whole-heartedly. This established a precedent for the treatment of rebel towns in future Italian expeditions.

Frederick began his southward march early in May 1155. He entered Romagna, stopped for a few days at Bologna, where his relations with the citizens proved amicable, then crossed the Apennines into Tuscany. At some point during this journey he sent a letter to his brother-in-law Landgrave Ludwig (ii) of Thuringia (his sister's husband) stating that all was going well and that he and his army were unharmed and victorious.[12] On 8 June he met the new pope, Adrian iv, at Sutri, 45 kilometres (28 mi.) north of Rome. Otto of Freising described how, when the two met, the pope 'was received with the honour due to his office' and was given a deferential hearing when he complained about the disobedience of the Romans. He and the emperor spent several days in 'pleasant conversation as between a spiritual father and his son'.[13] Here the bishop was being, to say the least, disingenuous. In fact, other sources reveal that there was a blazing row. This was despite the envoys who had been shuttling back and forth between the two principals once the army had entered Tuscany (Anselm of Havelberg, newly nominated as Archbishop of Ravenna, had played a prominent part in these negotiations). The dispute was caused by a matter of protocol. It had become customary, so the Curia argued, that when pope and monarch met, the latter should show his deference by performing the so-called 'marshal service', walking beside the pope's horse and holding his stirrup – as Emperor Lothar had done when he first met Innocent ii. Frederick at first refused, which the pope said was an insult to St Peter, the patron of the Apostolic See. The king was persuaded to back down, but then there was argument both about what exactly he should do – should he lead the horse by the bridle or hold the stirrup, and if so which one? – and more importantly about why he should do this. Was this ceremony an obligation that he *had* to perform, which implied subordination and even that he was a papal vassal, or was it something that he was *prepared* to do voluntarily, as an act of courtesy towards the spiritual leader of Christendom? The issue might seem petty, but contemporaries set great store by such ceremonies, which expressed abstract concepts in visual form. (How bishops were to be invested had been a similarly contentious issue a generation earlier.) And once the ceremony was performed, with Frederick still insisting that he was doing this of his own free will, Pope Adrian immediately demanded that he should invade the Kingdom of Sicily *before* he came to Rome to receive his imperial coronation. The German princes, however, flatly refused. They claimed that they were coming to the end of their resources, and were anxious to proceed to the coronation, and then return home.

There was still one more obstacle before Frederick could receive the imperial crown. A delegation from the Roman Senate, as the city council liked to style itself, arrived and tried to impose conditions before they would allow the king to enter Rome. They demanded a substantial sum of money, claiming that this was customary, and that he swear to respect the city's privileges. Otto of Freising gave a lengthy account of these negotiations, in the form of complex rhetorical speeches by both the Roman envoys and the king, but he was not present on the expedition and these were his own invention after the event. The one point in his account that rings true is when Frederick, in a bad temper, abruptly interrupted the Italians, and refused to accede to their demands. While it was customary for large sums of money to be distributed to the audience at the coronation, this was, as with holding the papal stirrup, something that the new emperor *chose* to do and in no sense a condition for the ceremony to take place. Frederick had no intention of being held to ransom. And

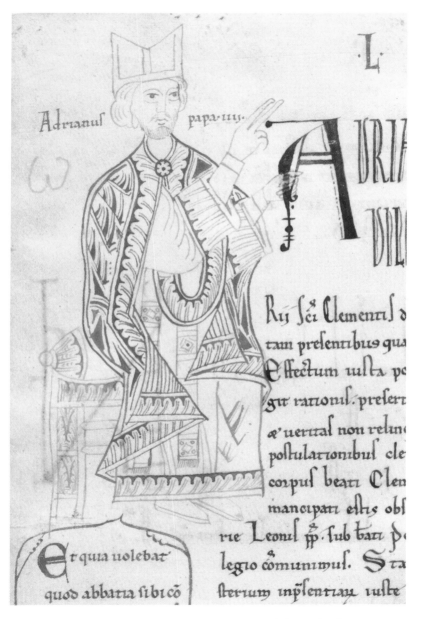

Pope Adrian IV depicted in the *Chronicon Casauriense* (Chronicle of Casauria), *c.* 1180.

confirming the city's privileges would be tantamount to recognizing the legitimacy of the Senate, which would infringe
Frederick's earlier agreement with the papacy and further damage
his already delicate relations with Adrian IV. The problem was
how to gain access to the Leonine City (the quarter of Rome to
the west of the Tiber) and to St Peter's, the traditional setting
for the imperial coronation, in the face of a potentially hostile
populace. Early in the morning of Saturday 18 June, Octavian,
cardinal priest of St Cecilia, who was both a native Roman and
Barbarossa's principal ally at the Curia, led the German troops
into the Leonine City. Once they had secured the area round St
Peter's, Frederick followed, to be met by the pope, who then
crowned him emperor.

Although taken by surprise, not least in that it would have
been more usual to have held the ceremony on a Sunday, and at
first unaware of what was going on, the Romans reacted angrily.
A disorderly mob crossed the bridge by the Castel St Angelo and
attacked the clergy and any Germans that they could find. The
emperor's troops, most of whom had by now retired to their camp
outside the walls, then re-entered the Leonine City and attacked
them. The battle was one-sided, for the Romans stood little
chance against these heavily armed and disciplined troops, and
hundreds were killed. The north German chronicler Helmold
of Bosau claimed that Henry the Lion took the leading role in
the fighting.[14]

After this bloodbath, there can have been no question of
lingering in Rome – though Pope Adrian to some extent restored
his standing with the citizens by persuading Frederick to release
the prisoners who had been taken during this battle. Frederick
lingered for the next three weeks in the hills to the east of Rome,
persuading the local towns to submit, although after some protest
by Adrian he agreed that their inhabitants should recognize the
pope as their lord, rather than him, albeit 'saving the rights of the

empire', which left him some potential leeway in the future. At some point – it is not clear whether this was before or after his coronation – he had at the pope's request handed Arnold of Brescia, whom he had captured, over to the papal prefect of the city, who promptly had the troublemaker executed. Then, in mid-July, with many of his men falling sick in the heat, Frederick turned north. Only one major incident marred the return journey, when the people of Spoleto first tried to avoid paying the *fodrum*, the customary render that was levied to support the imperial army, and then captured one of the emperor's Italian allies, Count Guido Guerra. After a brief battle the city was sacked. The army then crossed the Apennines further south than it had on its outward journey and around mid-August arrived at Ancona, where Frederick encountered some Byzantine envoys who offered a large monetary subsidy if he would now attack the Kingdom of Sicily. That can hardly have been a realistic possibility – the most that could be done was to send Abbot Wibald back to Constantinople with the envoys and allow some of the south Italian exiles who had accompanied his army to try to foment rebellion in their kingdom. By 7 September, after some skirmishing in the territory of Verona, the army had reached Trento, in the foothills of the Alps, arriving back in Germany a few days later. On 13 October 1155 the emperor held a diet (an assembly or parliament) at Regensburg.

Frederick had secured his imperial coronation, which was more than his uncle had done, and he and his advisers, at least publicly, took an optimistic view of what had been achieved. Hence in his letter to Ludwig of Thuringia, before his encounter with the pope, Frederick had claimed, 'we have concluded all our affairs in the Lombard region to our satisfaction,' and 'we are directing our victorious eagles towards the City to receive the ultimate distinction of our crown.' Otto of Freising said that the emperor had returned 'victorious, renowned and triumphant'.[15]

Yet the first Italian expedition had been, at best, a very partial success. Frederick had probably a much clearer idea of the problems that restoration of effective imperial rule in northern Italy would entail and of who his potential allies might be. He had established good relations with several of the smaller Lombard cities whose leaders were apprehensive about the expansionist ambitions of Milan. Most of the Italian cities had paid the *fodrum*, however reluctantly. But the examples made of various rebel towns had been ineffectual – Tortona, for example, was reoccupied and rebuilding began within a few months of its destruction. Milan was openly hostile, the loyalty of other important cities like Verona was doubtful, and the Milanese had not been in any way deterred from trying to impose their rule over the smaller neighbouring towns. Furthermore, it was already clear that Frederick's high sense of his own authority was going to make relations with the papacy difficult. Nor was he any closer to overcoming the Kingdom of Sicily, and the pope must have begun to doubt whether there was any useful contribution that he might make to achieving that.

Worse indeed was to come. In less than a year after Frederick's return to Germany there was a rapprochement between the papacy and the Kingdom of Sicily. Admittedly in the intervening period the kingdom had been seriously under threat. Just as Frederick was crossing the Alps, the new king, William, fell seriously ill and was rumoured to have died. This sparked a major rebellion in the mainland provinces, headed by the returning exiles with the aid of a Byzantine force that landed in Apulia. Pope Adrian encouraged the rebels and went to Benevento, the papal enclave in southern Italy, to assist, and perhaps coordinate, their efforts. Yet as soon as King William recovered his health, he launched a devastating counteroffensive. The rebels were driven out, one of their main leaders, Prince Robert of Capua, was captured and ended his days in a dungeon in Palermo, and the Greek army was annihilated near Brindisi in May 1156. Trapped in Benevento, Pope Adrian decided to make peace, and in June he and the Sicilian negotiators concluded a treaty which not only recognized the kingdom's existence and frontiers, and regulated its status as a papal vassal, but put an end to almost all the ecclesiastical problems that had bedevilled relations with the papacy since 1139. From being a rebel and pariah, the Kingdom of Sicily had now become a papal ally. Five months later the king of Sicily concluded a commercial treaty with Genoa, one of the maritime cities whose shipping the emperor would need if he were ever to launch a serious attack on Sicily. And less than two years after that a peace was agreed between Sicily and the Byzantine Empire – Emperor Manuel having decided that further attempts to destabilize the kingdom would be fruitless. The alliances that had been in place for some twenty years had unravelled.

Frederick's return to Germany had also revealed problems. Otto of Freising indeed complained that 'during the time that the prince was in Italy, practically the entire transalpine realm felt the absence of its head, being torn by uprisings and thrown into confusion by fire and sword and open warfare.'[16] One suspects hyperbole here – Frederick had, after all, been away for only eleven months. But there clearly had been some trouble. In his letter from Italy to the Landgrave of Thuringia, Frederick had ordered him to deal with a man called Hugo of Merchesleiben and make him cease his *infestationes* (raids, robberies, outrages?). The most serious issue that had emerged in his absence was a feud in the Rhineland between Archbishop Arnold of Mainz and Hermann, Count Palatine of the Rhine, which threatened to destabilize the region. Both parties were found guilty of arson and pillage, although the archbishop was spared punishment out of respect for his office. The count and his chief supporters were forced to undergo ritual humiliation in public.[17] The major problem that still required resolution was that of the Duchy of

Bavaria. Shortly before the expedition had left for Italy a decision in principle had been taken to restore Henry the Lion to
his father's duchy. But there had been no time to put this into
effect, and the problem was how to reconcile Henry Jasomirgott
to the loss of his position and status. That Frederick still intended to make the change is suggested by a privilege for the
monastery of Benediktbeuern that he issued while he was near
Bologna in May 1155, which said, 'If the duke of Bavaria shall
be led by love of the abbot and brothers, or wish to please them,
by restoring the various ancient revenues that have been taken
away, the duke succeeding him shall not infringe this.'[18] Furthermore, Frederick had some influential supporters among the
Bavarian nobility, for both Otto of Wittelsbach, Count Palatine
of Bavaria, and Count Berthold of Andechs had accompanied
him to Italy. Shortly before he finally reached an agreement with
Duke Henry, the emperor was staying at one of Count Otto's
castles. The eventual settlement was laid out in a privilege, drawn
up at Regensburg in September 1156, which was witnessed by
an unusually large number of the great men of the Reich, and
especially of Bavaria. Henry of Babenberg agreed to surrender
the Duchy of Bavaria to Henry the Lion. But in return the East
March of Bavaria, his own ancestral land, was to be entirely independent of Bavaria and in future to be a duchy (the Duchy of
Austria), which was to be held hereditarily. Should Henry lack
children, he could designate whomever he wished as his heir. He
should possess a monopoly of justice within his duchy, would only
have to attend imperial courts in Bavaria and not elsewhere and
should only owe military service to the emperor in the regions
immediately adjoining Austria.[19] In effect, therefore, not only
had a new duchy been created for Henry Jasomirgott, but it was
to be semi-independent of imperial authority. Otto of Freising,
who was one of those who witnessed the privilege to his brother,
said that Frederick thought this his finest achievement so far,

'that, without the shedding of blood, he was able to bring to friendly relations princes of the realm so mighty and so closely related to himself'.[20]

Frederick's other achievement during 1156 was that he got married, something absolutely essential since he needed an heir and his previous marriage to Adela of Vohburg had been dissolved three years earlier. There had, after that, been some rather desultory negotiations to obtain a Byzantine princess as his new bride and thereby cement the alliance between the two empires, but these had come to nothing. At Würzburg in June 1156 he married Beatrice, the daughter and heir of Count Rainald (III) of Burgundy, who had died some years earlier. She was still a child – probably no more than eleven or twelve – and the couple's first child, a daughter, was only born in 1163. But she was from a prestigious family – Pope Calixtus II had been her great-uncle – and possession of the County of Burgundy, the region around Besançon, gave Frederick a significant foothold within the wider kingdom of Burgundy, which was nominally part of the empire but had largely escaped from its rulers' control. Nor does the appointment at the start of the reign of the Duke of Zähringen as viceroy seem to have achieved anything. After his marriage Frederick devoted considerable attention to Burgundy, visiting the region nine times between 1157 and 1178. The marriage was successful. Unlike his first wife, Beatrice was regularly named alongside Frederick in his charters, and she seems to have accompanied him on most of his travels. And although several of their children died in infancy, five sons grew to adulthood.

Much of the next two years was devoted to preparations for a second and much larger Italian expedition. Frederick also turned his attention to relations with neighbouring kingdoms. Some of these were purely diplomatic – establishing friendly relations with Henry II of England, for example, who sent envoys, with gifts and a letter filled with obsequious flattery, to a diet held at Würzburg in September 1157. (At the same meeting some Byzantine envoys were given a much brusquer reception, but relations with the Eastern Empire were already deteriorating by then.[21]) But Frederick was also concerned to extend his influence, and if possible his overlordship, over the states to the east and north of Germany. He invaded Poland in August 1157 and forced Duke Boleslaw to appear before him as a suppliant, in a carefully choreographed ritual of submission. The duke also promised to pay him a significant sum of money, in lieu of the customary tribute that he had previously failed to pay, and more to the princes, and to take part in the forthcoming Italian expedition. In January 1158 he granted Duke Vladislav of Bohemia, who had earlier helped to broker the agreement with Henry Jasomirgott, a royal crown 'in return for distinguished service and devotion both from him and all the Bohemians'.[22] More to the point Vladislav pledged to take part in the Italian expedition, and unlike the Polish duke he fulfilled that promise. Frederick also interfered, albeit at long range, in the succession dispute raging in Denmark, and the eventual victor, King Waldemar, sent envoys to request the emperor to invest him as king and promised to swear fealty to Frederick when the latter returned from Italy. In addition, King Géza II of Hungary gave the emperor both money and troops for the expedition in return for Frederick withdrawing his support from the king's exiled brother, who had sought his throne. These military reinforcements were obviously useful, and the new king of Bohemia and his men were indeed to play a prominent part in the second Italian expedition. Tribute – if it was paid – was equally valuable in helping to finance that operation. But also the fealty of kings and other princes, and the exercise of his prerogative by creating a new king, showed Frederick genuinely acting as an emperor – a super-monarch whom other rulers obeyed, or should do. Frederick undoubtedly believed this himself, but so too did others. In the contemporary *Play of Antichrist* other monarchs – including significantly the 'king of the Greeks' (as the Byzantine emperor was demeaningly described) – all recognized the western emperor's superior status: 'We recognise your imperial sovereignty; We follow your command whole-heartedly.'[23]

The event that was, however, most significant during this period, certainly in its long-term repercussions, took place in a court at Besançon in October 1157, during Frederick's first visit to the lordship in Burgundy that he had acquired through his marriage. There a papal embassy, headed by the chancellor of the Roman Church, Cardinal Rolando Bandinelli, brought a letter from Pope Adrian, which was translated and read out to the assembly by the emperor's new chancellor, Rainald of Dassel. In this, the pope complained about the detention of the Danish archbishop Eskil of Lund, as he had been travelling through Germany (which may indeed have been on Frederick's order). But what caused great offence was an incidental reference in the letter to the pope having conferred the imperial title on Frederick as a *beneficium*. While this word was ambiguous in medieval Latin, it was understood to mean, or Rainald translated it in this sense, that the pope was here claiming to have granted the empire as a fief (*beneficium*, 'benefice', rather than as elsewhere *feudum*, was the usual term for this in Germany). Hence he was claiming that the emperor was his vassal and that the imperial title was the pope's to confer or not as he saw fit. The result was uproar, for not just the emperor but the German princes were irate. Cardinal Rolando then made matters worse by tactlessly asking, 'from whom then does he have the empire if not from our lord the Pope?' In response, Frederick's ally and friend Otto of Wittelsbach drew his sword and threatened the legates. The emperor stepped in to protect them before blood was shed, but he was still furious. The legates were told to leave his court immediately and to return to Rome. Before they departed their quarters were searched, and further incriminating letters were allegedly discovered. Frederick addressed an angry letter to the pope, in which he claimed that the whole incident had been a deliberate attempt to undermine his authority.

Both emperor and princes considered that this imperial status was derived from his original election as king. This was the constitutive act of appointment, while the imperial coronation was only a declarative one, a confirmation of his existing position. The emperor's power stemmed from the princes, whose choice had in turn been guided by God and not the pope. (The imperial chancery indeed sometimes called the ruler emperor even before his coronation in Rome, as had also been the case during Conrad III's reign.) Frederick's subsequent letter of complaint to the pope was blunt and to the point. He cited the words of St Peter: 'fear God and honour the king,'[24] and continued, 'whosoever says that we received the imperial crown as a benefice from the lord pope contradicts the divine ordinance and the doctrine of Peter and is guilty of a lie.' The pope in turn responded by complaining about the 'blasphemies' that chancellor Rainald and Count Otto, in particular, had directed against the legates and the Roman Church, and in response a letter sent in the name of the German bishops, no doubt at the emperor's prompting, accused the legates of trying to upset the established order in the kingdom and reiterated that the emperor's authority stemmed from God as mediated through his election, not from the pope.[25] At this point, with the emperor about to enter Italy once more, Pope Adrian decided not to prolong the dispute any further and sent two other cardinals as legates with a much more emollient missive, in which he claimed that his intention in the letter read out at Besançon was to say no more than that the conferment of the imperial title was a 'benefit' or 'blessing' from the pope. The crisis was thus, at least temporarily, averted. But, despite the pope's subsequent climbdown, a stark contrast between his conception of the emperor's authority and that of Frederick had become clear. It was to become very significant in the years to come.

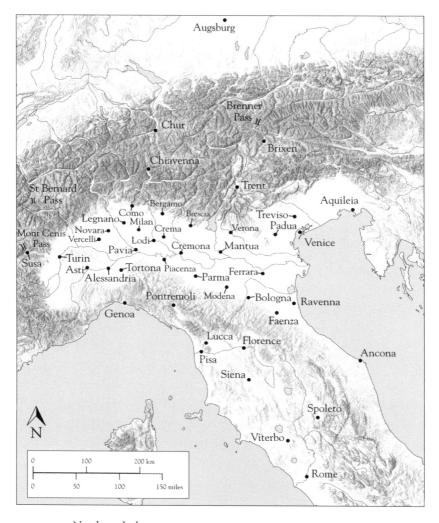

Northern Italy.

THREE

Italy, 1158–78

Frederick entered Italy for the second time in June 1158. For the next twenty years his attempts to enforce his authority south of the Alps were to be his primary concern. During this period he made four expeditions to Italy, two of them very extended (June 1158 to August 1162, October 1163 to the end of September 1164, October 1166 to early March 1168 and September 1174 to July 1178). In all, therefore, during these twenty years he spent just over half his time in Italy, the greater part of which was in Lombardy. We may well ask *why* he was so concerned with Italy, particularly since that region had been largely neglected by his predecessors.

In part, of course, it was that neglect that explained why Frederick was now so determined to restore imperial authority in the Italian kingdom. Given how the independence and self-confidence of the northern cities had developed over the previous half-century, it was for the emperor now a case of 'use it or lose it'. Otto of Freising shrewdly commented,

> They [the Italian cities] scarcely if ever respect the prince to whom they should display the voluntary deference of obedience, or willingly perform what they have sworn by the integrity of their laws, unless they sense his authority in the power of his great army.[1]

Frederick was now about to display that power. Italy was, in his eyes, just as much his kingdom as was Germany, and he was therefore entitled actually to rule over it and not just reign in theory as an absentee monarch. Indeed, it was not just his right but also his duty properly to exercise that authority which God had given him, and not to abandon the rights that his predecessors had once exercised and that his successors would expect to possess. He also clearly thought that the defiance shown by some cities in 1154–5 was not just disobedience to their lawful ruler but an insult to his honour and reputation that needed to be punished. There were, in addition, some very practical reasons why exercising more direct rule in the Italian kingdom would be advantageous. Although Germany's economy was growing in the twelfth century and the country was becoming richer, it remained less developed than that of Italy. German towns, with the possible exception of Cologne, were still relatively small, and trade, while probably expanding, was on a lesser scale than in Italy. Not only were Italian towns growing in size but they were increasing in wealth, not least through the developing Mediterranean trade of the maritime cities, which filtered back into the inland areas, on which the ports drew for foodstuffs, raw materials and (increasingly) artisanal manufactures. The Italian economy was also significantly more monetarized than that of Germany. It is notable that in a schedule of imperial property that was drawn up in the early years of Frederick's reign, and probably soon after his accession, the German estates provided food renders, but half of those listed in Italy furnished cash rents, which amounted in total to the substantial sum of 5,600 marks (almost £3,800).[2] And by recovering former imperial property in Italy that had been alienated, by recovering and exploiting potentially lucrative regalian rights over tolls, minting, justice and fisheries, and by exacting tribute to punish those cities that had proved recalcitrant, the emperor could enjoy a substantial extra income. Thus Verona, whose men had harassed Frederick's army in 1155, sent its bishop to his court a year later to offer not just an apology, but a large sum of money to recover his grace. The prospect of extra income was all the more important to Frederick because in his early years his own lands in Germany were quite limited, not least because he had had to make provision for his cousin Frederick of Rothenburg, whom he had displaced as ruler from the Staufen family lands in Swabia.

The army that entered Italy in June 1158 was much larger than the one Frederick had led three and a half years earlier. Almost fifty lay and ecclesiastical princes – that is, those who were direct vassals of the emperor – accompanied him, as opposed to twenty on the earlier expedition. These included the new king of Bohemia and most of the really important figures from Germany: the dukes of Austria, Carinthia, Dalmatia, Swabia and Zähringen; the margraves of Baden, Lausitz, Meißen (these last two brothers, from the powerful Wettin family) and Vohburg; the emperor's half-brother Conrad, now Count Palatine of the Rhine (Swabia); the archbishops of Cologne, Mainz, Magdeburg and Trier; a dozen other German bishops; and Bishop Daniel of Prague, whose presence was deemed especially useful since he spoke fluent Italian. Otto of Wittelsbach, Count Palatine of Bavaria, and the chancellor Rainald had been sent ahead to prepare the way by securing the submission and assistance of as many cities and Italian nobles as possible. In some cases there had been negotiation to secure their adherence. It is probable, for example, that Henry Jasomirgott's participation had been part of the agreement creating his new duchy in 1156, even if this was not expressly mentioned in the privilege creating it. King Vladislav of Bohemia faced some grumbling among his nobles, who complained that they had not been consulted before he had offered to go to Italy, but he bullied or shamed most of them into taking part. Archbishop Arnold of Mainz had certainly been reluctant and had attempted to plead old age and ill health to avoid taking part, but the emperor was having none of this, especially since the archbishop had not come to Italy in 1154–5 and had then caused trouble in Frederick's absence, as we have seen. Arnold then faced difficulties with his own *ministeriales* and the citizens of Mainz, many of whom were reluctant to contribute to his expenses. But in the end he provided a force of 140 knights at his own expense. They were joined by the troops of various of the cities that favoured Frederick, especially those that had suffered from the attempts of Milan either to subordinate them to its rule or to expand into their territory – hence Como, Cremona, Lodi, Novara and Pavia all furnished significant contingents, as did Bergamo, which hoped for the emperor's assistance against its aggressive neighbour, Brescia. A Milanese chronicler said that Frederick's army had 15,000 knights and 'infantry without number', and while this must surely be a very significant over-estimate the imperial army still outnumbered the forces available to Milan several times over.[3] So large was the force coming from Germany that while the emperor, his immediate family and the Bohemians crossed the Alps by the Brenner, as he had done in 1154, other sections of the army used no fewer than three other Alpine passes. Berthold of Zähringen, with his own troops and those from Alsace and Burgundy, crossed by the Great St Bernard in the west.

Milan was always the main target of the expedition. The surrender of Milan would secure the submission of the whole of western Lombardy, and the city was already under sentence of outlawry after its resistance to the 1154–5 expedition. The imperial army moved swiftly, forced a crossing of the river Adda – the main physical barrier protecting Milanese territory – and laid siege to the city in early August. There was some sharp fighting – one Austrian count was captured and beheaded outside Milan as the imperial columns were approaching the city, and its territory was systematically ravaged by the besiegers, with the enthusiastic participation of the local enemies of the Milanese. After a month's close siege, with no prospect of relief and with food supplies running short, the Milanese surrendered in early September, following several days' negotiations in which the king of Bohemia and Henry of Austria had acted as intermediaries. The terms were severe, but the surrender was still on terms rather than unconditional. The Milanese consuls were forced to make a public submission to the emperor, barefoot and wearing penitential clothing, and handing their swords to him, while their spokesman proclaimed their repentance and asked for forgiveness. All Milanese over the age of fourteen were to swear fealty to the emperor, three hundred hostages were to be handed over as pledges that the surrender agreement would be observed, and a fine of 9,000 marks would be paid in three instalments. All prisoners whom the city was holding were to be released immediately. The independence and security of Como and Lodi, the two principal victims of Milanese aggression, were guaranteed. But the current consuls could remain in place until their term of office had expired, Milan could continue to levy dues from its traditional territory – though not from neighbouring towns which had historically been independent – and provision was made for the Milanese hostages eventually to be released once the terms of the surrender had been completely fulfilled. It must have seemed, at least to the emperor and his advisers, that justice had been tempered with mercy, and that this agreement provided the basis for preserving the peace of Lombardy thereafter. In the event it lasted little over seven months.

After the surrender of Milan, Frederick had allowed some of his army to return home, in particular the king of Bohemia, the dukes of Austria and Zähringen and the Archbishop of Mainz and their troops. With the rest of his force he moved to stamp out any lingering embers of resistance elsewhere, particularly from Verona, and to exact oaths of fealty and hostages from other cities. In November he held an assembly at Roncaglia, which was attended by representatives from all the major cities, including Milan. While Frederick presided over a number of legal cases, showing himself as the dispenser of justice in the region, the primary purpose of the meeting was to define and reclaim the imperial *regalia*, and for the emperor's exercise of these rights to be recognized by the representatives of the cities. To this end Frederick had summoned the four leading judges and law teachers of Bologna (already the pre-eminent centre of legal study in Italy) to advise him. They in turn requested that judges from other cities be co-opted. The proceedings thus had at least the appearance of consultation, and it was stressed that the emperor was not seeking to extend his rights but to recover those to which he was historically entitled, and that anybody who possessed written title from previous rulers to regalian rights would be allowed to retain these. Nevertheless, Rahewin, who was an eyewitness of this assembly, thought that the recovery of the *regalia* would bring in an annual revenue of £30,000. While this figure was surely a considerable overestimate, he clearly meant that they were potentially extremely lucrative. (The Genoese, for example, although very reluctant to surrender any regalian rights that they had held, eventually agreed to make a one-off payment of 1,200 marks to stave off trouble and gave vague promises about future restitution.) Frederick then went on to repeat his earlier decrees about fiefs and to promulgate a general land peace and detailed provisions for the upholding of law and order. One of these provisions certainly had a wider political intent:

> We also absolutely forbid that there be associations and any sworn brotherhoods, in and outside the cities . . .

whether between city and city, person and person, or a city
and a person, and we abolish those formed in the past.[4]

This would prevent cities forming alliances against the emperor.

Frederick's first action after the Roncaglia council was to
sanction the refoundation of Lodi on a new site that would be
more defensible against Milanese aggression – and also to reward
a community that had been consistently loyal to him.[5] Afterwards
he travelled first into Piedmont, where he spent Christmas, and
then in the new year into Emilia–Romagna, where he reasserted
imperial ownership over the lands that had once been held by
Countess Matilda of Tuscany (d. 1115). This was another issue
that would potentially make relations with the pope difficult.
On her death Matilda had bequeathed her extensive lordship
to the papacy, but neither Henry v nor subsequent emperors
had recognized the validity of this grant. These lands had been
held from the empire; they were not therefore Matilda's to give
away without the emperor's permission. Frederick had previously conferred the revenues from these lands on his uncle
Welf vi, but he had remained in Germany and failed to exercise
his rights, and so now the emperor sought to take these properties into his own possession. In addition, he despatched a
group of trusted subordinates, including the chancellor and the
Bishop of Prague, to visit the cities of Lombardy and Emilia to
supervise the appointment of new *podestà*, the chief executive
magistrates of the cities. It appears that they were not trying to
impose the emperor's own candidates for these posts but they
were emphasizing that the magistrates' authority derived from
him – and potentially screening out those who might be hostile
to the emperor.

In the early months of 1159 it must therefore have seemed
as if the recovery of imperial authority in northern Italy was
well advanced, but this process was now derailed by renewed

hostilities with Milan. The contemporary chronicler from that city suggested three reasons for this, all of them in his eyes intrusions by the emperor into Milanese rights that were in breach of the earlier surrender agreement. First, he had ordered the defences of Crema, Milan's principal ally, to be razed, allegedly after receiving a bribe of 15,000 marks from the men of Cremona. Second, German officers were levying dues, including the *fodrum*, on men in the eastern part of the Milanese *contado*, near the river Adda. Third, Rainald the chancellor and Count Otto of Wittelsbach arrived to supervise the election of a new *podestà* in Milan. The inhabitants were infuriated, a riot broke out and the two imperial envoys fled the city. From that day, the chronicler said, Rainald was determined to destroy the city.[6] Otto Morena, the pro-imperial chronicler from Lodi, gave a different interpretation of these events. Despite the threats to his officers, first by the people of Crema and then by the Milanese, Frederick remained calm and decided not to retaliate. It was only when, in April 1159, the Milanese captured a castle that he had garrisoned with German troops the previous year, and then in May launched an attack on Lodi, that the emperor decided that he had had enough.[7] Otto probably exaggerated Frederick's patience – other sources suggest that the Milanese were formally outlawed while the emperor was at Bologna in April. But Frederick had been careful to observe the legal niceties; the Milanese had been summoned several times to appear at his court, and the advice of Bolognese jurists had been sought before the sentence was passed.

One reason why the emperor may have chosen not to react too hastily to Milanese provocation was that having dismissed part of his army, he was short of troops. Much of the fighting in the early stages of this renewed campaign against Milan was done by soldiers from the emperor's Italian allies, especially Cremona, Lodi and Pavia. Probably soon after hostilities recommenced, Frederick sent Rainald of Dassel back to Germany to muster reinforcements and formally take possession of the archbishopric of Cologne, to which he had recently been elected.[8] The empress and Henry the Lion arrived with a substantial army in July, Welf vi with a further three hundred knights in September and Rainald with others in October. The early stages of the campaign had been limited to a series of raids and counter-raids, but from July onwards its focal point was the siege of Crema, which had been begun, significantly, by the men of Cremona, but which was soon heavily reinforced by German troops as these became available. Despite this, the siege lasted for six months of increasingly bitter fighting. Crema, strongly fortified and with its defenders reinforced by Milanese soldiers, proved a tough nut to crack, despite the imperial army having the services of an experienced siege engineer from the kingdom of Jerusalem. It only surrendered on 26 January 1160. The severe terms on which Frederick insisted reflected how difficult the siege had been. While guaranteed their lives, the inhabitants had to evacuate the town and were permitted to take with them only what they themselves could carry. Crema was then looted; the men of Lodi did their best to overthrow the walls while those of Cremona burned the houses.

While this campaign was under way, Frederick's relations with Pope Adrian had remained problematic. The pope complained about the exaction of the *fodrum*, which imperial agents may have been levying in central Italy in lands to which the papacy laid claim. He objected to attempts to recover regalian rights held by bishops and abbeys – to which presumably they could not show title. He told Frederick not to interfere in a dispute between Brescia and Bergamo – here clearly interfering in a matter which pertained to the emperor. He also refused to allow the appointment of the emperor's favoured candidate to the now vacant archbishopric of Ravenna – Archbishop Anselm having died in

August 1158. The emperor, meanwhile, was taking control of the disputed lands once owned by Countess Matilda, opening negotiations with the Roman Senate (which infuriated the pope), complaining about alleged papal exactions from the Church in Germany – in a not very subtle bid for the support of churchmen in the Reich – and also alleging that the Church's peace agreement with Sicily was in contravention of its earlier agreement with the empire at Konstanz. There were some attempts at mediation, in particular by Cardinal Octavian of St Cecilia, the emperor's ally at the Curia, and Bishop Eberhard of Bamberg, but relations were still very poor when Adrian died on 1 September 1159. The consequences of his death were momentous.

The resulting papal election was disputed. After considerable discussion, a majority of the cardinals chose the chancellor, Rolando Bandinelli, as the new pope. But a minority, and to begin with at least a not entirely negligible one, elected Octavian, and his supporters moved quickly to have him enthroned as pope, with the pontifical name of Victor iv. After being besieged for some time in St Peter's by Octavian's supporters, the cardinals who backed Rolando succeeded in escaping and he was consecrated as Pope Alexander iii on 20 September. Two weeks later, rather belatedly, Victor iv was consecrated. Both popes proceeded to proclaim the legitimacy of their election and to denounce the wicked attempts of the other candidate to steal the papal throne.

The problem here was that there were no canonical rules for a disputed papal election. It was still assumed that with God's aid the cardinals would unanimously agree on the best candidate – even though an earlier disputed election in 1130 had led to a long schism. Then the college of cardinals had been split more or less down the middle. In 1159 it seems that initially fourteen cardinals voted for Alexander and nine for Victor, although two or three of the latter subsequently changed sides. But Victor's supporters claimed, as those of Innocent II had done in 1130, that they represented the 'wiser party' among the cardinals, that the clergy of Rome were overwhelmingly in favour of their candidate and that he had been publicly enthroned first. They argued that those who had voted for Rolando ought at this point to have fallen into line behind the 'true' pope.

Frederick himself cannot have been aware of these proceedings until after the event, but his trusted friend Otto of Wittelsbach was in Rome as his envoy, and once Octavian had been proclaimed pope he worked enthusiastically for his cause. Otto was, of course, well aware that Octavian was a long-standing ally of Frederick and had worked hard for good relations between papacy and empire, while as a result of the incident at Besançon in 1157 the emperor loathed Rolando, who had also been one of the architects of the treaty with the king of Sicily that the imperial court so disliked. Nevertheless, Frederick's initial reaction, once he was apprised of the double election, was superficially neutral. He immediately despatched messengers to other monarchs informing them of what had happened and requesting that they make no precipitous decision in favour of either claimant. He also announced that a council would meet at Pavia in late January, just over three months later, to examine the two candidates and their cases and to decide who the true pope was. To this end a general summons called the bishops of Christendom to attend – although predictably almost all of those who did come were from Italy or Germany, some of the latter already being present with the imperial army. In theory this was a Church council, and the bishops present would decide the outcome. But it was to be held in the emperor's presence and many must have suspected who would have the decisive voice. Alexander's reaction was immediate. He was the legitimate pope, and Frederick, as a layman, however exalted, had no right to summon him to a council. The emperor's position as protector of the Roman

Church required him to be obedient to the pope and did not entitle him to interfere in Church affairs. So when the council finally convened, two weeks late so that the siege of Crema could be completed, Victor attended and his cardinals presented his case that he was 'the true and Catholic pope'. Alexander did not and denounced the illegitimacy of the whole proceedings. The council, encouraged by speeches from, among others, archbishop-elect Rainald, therefore predictably declared Victor to be the only true pope, which he had shown by humbly submitting to the council's judgement. The emperor, who had tactfully not so far spoken, then concurred. As Victor was escorted to a further enthronement ceremony, he performed the marshal service, holding his stirrup – the ceremony which had caused such trouble in 1155.[9] Envoys were despatched to France, England, Hungary and other kingdoms to announce the Church's decision.

The schism that resulted from the disputed election lasted for eighteen years. Frederick remained obstinately loyal both to Victor, who died in 1164, and to the two popes elected to succeed him (Paschal III, 1164–8, and Calixtus III, 1168–78). For the most part, although with a few significant exceptions, the churchmen of Germany supported these 'popes', or 'antipopes' as they were later deemed. So too did ecclesiastics from those north Italian cities that supported the empire, and from much of central Italy. But almost nobody else did. Frederick's diplomatic campaign in support of Victor IV was a resounding failure, while that of Alexander was shrewdly directed and remarkably effective. The kings of England, France, Jerusalem and Sicily, and their churchmen, almost immediately recognized Alexander III and they continued to do so after Alexander was forced to take refuge in France in 1162. The various Spanish rulers hesitated for a little while, but the kings of both León and Castile had recognized Alexander before the end of 1160, and the king of Portugal by 1162. The Byzantine emperor was negotiating with

Alexander by late 1160, and their later relations were to be surprisingly warm. Admittedly, the king of Denmark, who needed Frederick's support and recognition, at first acknowledged Victor as pope, but by the time of the latter's death he had switched sides. And after 1167 even Frederick's valued ally the king of Bohemia and his bishops did the same. The schism also greatly complicated Frederick's attempts to rule in Italy. Those cities that opposed Frederick were encouraged by Pope Alexander to combat this enemy of the Church, whom Alexander had excommunicated in March 1160. Other cities whose clergy and counsellors supported Alexander, like Genoa and Venice, inevitably ended up opposing Frederick, even if to begin with they did not openly come out against him.

After the council of Pavia, Frederick once again disbanded the bulk of his army. Henry the Lion, Frederick of Rothenburg and most of the German bishops returned home. For the next year the emperor once more had to rely primarily on the troops of those Lombard cities who supported his rule. The fighting was a matter of raid and counter-raid, with neither side strong enough to secure a decisive advantage. Milanese territory was periodically ravaged, and Frederick attempted to blockade the city by preventing the importation of foodstuffs from its allies, notably Piacenza and Brescia. Reinforcements from Germany only arrived in April 1161, led by Frederick's brother-in-law, the Landgrave of Thuringia, his half-brother Conrad, his cousin Frederick of Rothenburg and the Archbishop of Cologne. The last two brought six hundred and five hundred knights respectively, although most of these only stayed for about six months. There was in addition a smaller Bohemian contingent, led by a brother of the king. The Archbishop of Trier and no fewer than twelve other German bishops were also in Frederick's entourage during the summer of 1161. With his forces now appreciably more formidable, Frederick was able to conduct a much more aggressive campaign. Milan was closely blockaded, and the fields round the city repeatedly laid waste, vines cut down and other foodstuffs taken or spoiled. A diploma of Frederick drawn up early in June was issued 'before the gates of the city of Milan, in the time of ravaging'.[10] Despite the return of some troops to Germany, over the winter of 1161–2 the blockade was tightened still further. Garrisons were established at key points guarding the roads and men caught bringing food to Milan had their right hands amputated. Cruel as this treatment was, it was effective – the flow of supplies dropped off and prices within Milan rose dramatically. This in turn caused internal dissension in the city, and the authorities decided that they had no alternative but to surrender. Their initial offer – that the emperor should select their *podestà*, and that the city wall be demolished and the moat filled in at six places – was rejected. Having been merciful in 1158 to little effect, the emperor now insisted on unconditional surrender. On 1 March 1162 the consuls appeared before the emperor to surrender the city and swear that they would in future obey his commands, and promised that they would have all the citizens swear likewise. The eventual terms resembled those exacted at Crema in January 1160. Four hundred hostages were to be handed over. The remainder of the population were given a week to evacuate the city, which was then to be destroyed. Most of the houses, and even the cathedral, were demolished or burned, although despite the best endeavours of Frederick's Italian allies the city walls were so solidly built that less damage was done than was hoped. The populace dispersed to other cities, or to villages in the Milanese *contado*. The archbishop, however, fled to join Pope Alexander, who was then at Genoa.

The destruction of Milan marked the high point of Frederick Barbarossa's rule in Italy. It was celebrated in Pavia on Easter Sunday, when Frederick had a solemn crown-wearing, and then after Mass in the cathedral he and the empress held a great banquet where they entertained many of the Italian bishops and nobles, and the consuls of all the pro-imperial cities, including, as he proudly recorded, Acerbo Morena, the *podestà* of Lodi, who had taken over his father's chronicle.[11] Other hostile cities soon submitted. Brescia, for example, agreed to receive a new *podestà* from the emperor, to have the city fortifications demolished and to surrender other strong points in its territory, and to pay a substantial fine. Piacenza and Bologna followed suit on similar terms. Genoa, despite its loyalty to Alexander III, agreed to provide a fleet should Frederick undertake an invasion of the Kingdom of Sicily. To reinforce the reality of imperial rule, many of the new officials appointed were German, although those cities that had distinguished themselves by their loyalty to the empire were permitted to choose their own magistrates. Frederick remained for a few months more in northern Italy, but with that kingdom now peaceful and obedient he crossed from Turin into Burgundy in August 1162, there to hold a council to shore up support for Victor IV and to attempt (unavailingly) to detach the French king, Louis VII, from the cause of Pope Alexander. He then made a long-overdue return to Germany.

Frederick returned to Italy in October 1163, having in the intervening period sent Rainald of Dassel and another German bishop, Hermann of Verden, to oversee his Italian administration. If we can believe Acerbo Morena, Rainald was very successful in extending direct imperial rule into Tuscany and the Romagna.[12] Quite why Frederick returned so soon is something of a mystery. Perhaps he simply wanted to ensure that the government of northern Italy was working effectively, and to reassure his allies there. His first action was to attend the foundation of the new cathedral of Lodi by Victor IV, for the building of which he gave a generous cash donation.[13] He then conducted various negotiations with both Pisans and Genoese concerning a forthcoming invasion of the Kingdom of Sicily, something which had

Lodi Cathedral, founded in 1163.

first been mooted a year earlier. The Pisans, who were more committed imperial supporters than the Genoese, had already started building new ships for this operation in the autumn of 1162. But when Frederick then met envoys from Genoa in February 1164 he was less enthusiastic, saying that he needed advice from his princes, who were not there, and at that point the projected expedition was abandoned. There had, anyway, never been any realistic prospect of such an ambitious operation being launched, because Frederick had entered Italy with only a very small army; apart from the Archbishop of Cologne and the bishops of Verden and Liège, who were already in Italy, the only major figures who accompanied him were Welf VI and the ever-loyal Otto of Wittelsbach, the latter's brother Archbishop Conrad of Mainz (who was soon to desert to the side of Alexander III), one of the Bohemian princes and the Abbot of Hersfeld. It would seem that the very considerable efforts made by the German princes and nobility during the previous Italian expedition had at least temporarily exhausted their enthusiasm, or their resources.

There were nevertheless two very significant developments during the later stages of this expedition. First, on 20 April 1164 Victor IV died at Lucca. Rainald of Dassel immediately arranged for the election of a successor, Guy of Crema, Cardinal priest of St Maria in Trastevere, who assumed the pontifical name Paschal III. There can have been no time for Frederick to be consulted, although it was surely unlikely that his trusted collaborator was acting against what he knew were the emperor's wishes. But Victor's death would have been a good moment to try to end the schism, especially since Alexander had already made overtures to Frederick seeking a negotiated solution. The choice of a new pope did little to assist the emperor, and some of those who had hitherto been loyal to Victor started to waver in their allegiance after his death. Second, during the spring of 1164 a renewed revolt broke out in eastern Lombardy. Three cities were involved – Padua, Verona and Vicenza – although they were encouraged and financed by Venice, which was by now covertly, if not yet openly, hostile to the emperor. Their revolt was caused by what were seen as the excessive exactions of the imperial officials who had been appointed to this region, and, if we can believe the contemporary biographer of Alexander III, the three cities formed a sworn alliance, a *societas* or league, to oppose the emperor. Frederick advanced against them in June 1164, but found his army outnumbered. Acerbo Morena noted that 'he had only a few Germans with him, and that the Lombards displayed no great enthusiasm for coming to his aid'. He retreated, resolving to recruit a much larger army of Germans for his next expedition.[14] These were, as we shall see, ominous developments.

Meanwhile, the cause of Alexander III had been gaining ground. During his stay in France, he had held a council at Tours in May 1163, attended, so his biographer claimed, by no fewer than 124 bishops and more than 400 abbots.[15] Even in exile he was clearly the pontiff whose authority was generally recognized. By August 1165 he was sufficiently confident to set off for Italy, and after a roundabout journey via Sicily, where he was welcomed with great distinction by the king, he returned to Rome in November. Four years earlier he had been forced to abandon the city through lack of support and the danger from Victor's partisans. Now he was welcomed back by the Romans and their Senate. While Frederick must have been anxious to return to Italy, given the unresolved rebellion in eastern Lombardy, it was probably the news of Alexander's return that spurred the decision to begin preparations for a fresh expedition. At a council at Nuremberg in February 1166 the princes agreed what wages should be paid to the knights who took part, although the emperor did not cross the Alps until the last week of October. As with the other expeditions, long and careful preparations were needed before departure. It may well have been in preparation for this expedition, Frederick's fourth to Italy, that Archbishop Rainald had a detailed schedule drawn up of the rights and customs of the *ministeriales* of the see of Cologne, which included provisions for the payment and equipment of those taking part in an Italian expedition.[16] There may also have been some reluctance on the part of those who were summoned. Bishop Hermann of Hildesheim, for example, paid four hundred marks to the emperor instead of serving in person. Archbishop Rainald, the emperor's principal adviser, naturally took part but brought with him only one hundred knights, compared to five hundred in 1161. This may suggest some disenchantment among the knights, or the strain placed on the archbishop's resources by repeated service in Italy.

The army that crossed the Alps in the last week of October 1166 was large, if probably not as numerous as on the 1158 expedition. It is also possible that some of those who can be identified in Italy during the next summer followed on later. Nevertheless, by then Frederick was accompanied by the three archbishops of Cologne, Mainz and Besançon; nine other bishops; the abbots of Fulda and Stavelot; the dukes of Swabia and Zähringen; Conrad the Count Palatine; Welf vi's son and heir; one of the Wettin margraves from eastern Saxony; two members of the Bohemian royal family; at least a dozen counts from all over the Reich; and the burgraves of Magdeburg and Nuremberg. A new feature was the hire of significant numbers of mercenaries, the so-called *Rotten* or *Brabançons*, which was probably intended to make up for any deficiencies in the German contingents.

The extent of dissatisfaction with German rule became clear soon after the emperor's arrival. Moving south from the Brenner pass, his army had to fight its way not just through the territory of Brescia, which had long been hostile, but also through that of Bergamo, hitherto an ally. Then, after Frederick arrived at Lodi in November, he received both individuals and delegations complaining about the exactions by his officials and their exploitation of their positions for their own profit. Frederick did at least listen to these complaints, but as the Lodi chronicler Otto Morena, hitherto an imperial supporter, noted, 'at first the emperor claimed that he did indeed greatly sympathise with them, but in the end he did nothing, appearing to treat the complaints of the Lombards with contempt and as having no value.' The Lombards, he said, having trusted the emperor to redress their grievances, now thought that the oppression by his officials was in accordance with his orders.[17] This proved to be a terrible misjudgement.

Frederick set off southwards in January 1167, marching through the Romagna, exacting large sums of money from its towns and taking hostages. The journey was slow, delayed first by the empress being heavily pregnant – she gave birth to her third son near Faenza in mid-February – and then by the siege of

Ancona, where the Byzantines, by now allies of Alexander III and thoroughly hostile to the western emperor, had installed a garrison, which took up most of May. Meanwhile a second section of the imperial army, led by the archbishops of Cologne and Mainz, marched through Tuscany and arrived at Tuscolo, 24 kilometres (15 mi.) southeast of Rome, at the end of May. There they inflicted a sharp defeat on a much larger Roman force. Frederick concluded a hurried agreement with the citizens of Ancona, who gave him money and hostages, and hastened to take advantage of the recent victory. He still only reached Rome in late July, and it took several days' siege before he forced an entry into the Leonine City on 29 July. Paschal III was enthroned in St Peter's the next day, and on 1 August he crowned Beatrice as empress – she and Frederick both subsequently wearing their crowns in state. The Romans now came to an agreement with the emperor, recognizing his lordship in return for his confirmation of the city's privileges and the existence of the Senate. But gratifying as all this must have been, the success was only partial since Pope Alexander had fled from the city to avoid capture, eventually taking refuge at Benevento under the protection of the king of Sicily. Furthermore, two or three days later a disastrous epidemic broke out in the imperial army, probably bacterial dysentery, brought on by poor sanitation, made worse by the heat and heavy rain and an infected water supply. The mortality was catastrophic. Among the leaders of the army who died in the next two weeks were Rainald of Dassel; four other bishops, one of whom was Daniel of Prague; Duke Frederick of Swabia; Dietrich the brother of the king of Bohemia; and seven counts. Others lingered ill for some time before succumbing, notably Welf VII, who died at Siena on 12 September, and the jurist and chronicler Acerbo Morena, also at Siena, where he had been lying ill for some weeks, on 18 October. Two more bishops subsequently died. Otto Morena estimated that more than 2,000 nobles and knights had died before the army reached Lombardy, and those who survived were in very poor health.[18]

The loss of much of his army would have been disastrous enough, but even as Frederick had been marching south towards Rome most of Lombardy had risen in rebellion. The first step had been taken in March 1167 when the four cities of Bergamo, Brescia, Cremona and Mantua concluded a sworn agreement to protect their liberties. Two of these cities, Bergamo and Cremona, had hitherto been conspicuously loyal to the emperor, and Mantua had never caused any trouble and had not joined the earlier league formed by nearby Verona in 1164. This group then allied with the Milanese, still dispersed in villages in the city's territory, and at the end of April the allies' troops escorted them back to their city, where rebuilding was started. Over the next few weeks Lodi, after some initial resistance, and Piacenza also joined the league. Some time later so too did Parma and Ferrara. By December, when the three cities of the Verona league formally joined the others, the alliance contained some sixteen cities. One of the key features was that the members of the league pledged peace one with another, and in particular Milan gave guarantees to its former enemies that it would not resume the aggressive practices that had earlier forced them to seek help from the emperor.

When Frederick and what was left of his army reached Pavia in mid-September – not without some difficulty and after surviving an ambush at Pontremoli on the coast road north of Pisa – the only three cities still loyal to him in the north were Pavia, Novara and Vercelli, although he still also had the valuable assistance of William of Montferrat and Guido of Biandrate, and of Pisa in Tuscany. But this was hardly enough to fight the combined forces of the Lombard League, particularly since Frederick had little option but to allow most of his remaining, and exhausted, German troops to return home. Over the winter he was steadily forced westwards until he fled over the Mont-Cenis

pass into Burgundy in early March 1168. According to the
Swabian chronicler Otto of St Blasien, admittedly writing forty
years later, he had been forced to escape in disguise from Susa,
the last town before the pass, leaving one of his knights to im-
personate him.[19] If true, this was an appropriately embarrassing
ending to a catastrophic expedition, during which imperial rule
in Lombardy had collapsed and, far from settling the papal schism
in favour of the imperial candidate, the cause of Alexander III
had become even stronger than it had been before, not least
with the death of the antipope Paschal in September 1168. And
Frederick had also lost his most trusted adviser and right-hand
man, Archbishop Rainald, whom, as he lamented in a letter he
sent to the administrators of the Cologne see informing them
of his death, had always served him loyally and put the welfare
of the empire ahead of his private interests: 'we have not found
anyone similar in our empire.'[20]

Frederick remained in Germany for the next six and a half
years, the longest continuous period he spent in the Reich in
his entire reign. Throughout this period Lombardy remained
under the control of the league, and two of the cities that had to
begin with remained loyal to the emperor, Novara and Vercelli,
eventually joined it. The league also inflicted significant military defeats on Frederick's aristocratic supporters the counts
of Biandrate and Montferrat. And the league's alliance with
the generally recognized pope was strengthened by the foundation of a new city in western Lombardy, which was given
the name Alessandria. By 1172 the Lombard League had 24
members. By this time too it was beginning to develop its own
organization, with presiding officials (*rectores*), written rules reg-
ulating its affairs, including the arbitration of disputes between
members, and its own assembly and seal. It also conducted a
common diplomacy. It had become considerably more than just
a military alliance. That the imperial cause in Italy was not

entirely shipwrecked was largely due to Christian of Buch, the Archbishop of Mainz, a singularly warlike prelate who was sent to Italy as the emperor's governor in 1171 and managed to retain control over most of Romagna, Tuscany and the Marche. Not the least of his achievements was his success in maintaining peace between the warring port cities of Pisa and Genoa and their allies.

Frederick himself did not return to Italy until September 1174. In the intervening period there was one significant change in policy. From soon after his return to Germany the emperor began to make tentative enquiries about finding a solution to the schism. These attempts were probably encouraged by the lack of enthusiasm for the last of the three imperialist antipopes, John of Struma (Calixtus III), who had been elected apparently without Frederick's knowledge, and whom the emperor himself did not know. Although the majority of the German episcopate remained loyal to Frederick, they were far less committed to this latest antipope than they had been to Victor IV at the start of the schism, and there was a growing feeling among churchmen on both sides that it was time to heal the rift in Christendom. Frederick himself was in contact with the abbots of Citeaux and Clairvaux, the two leading monasteries of the Cistercian order which had remained conspicuously loyal to Alexander, in 1169. Bishop Eberhard of Bamberg was sent to Italy to negotiate directly with Pope Alexander in 1170, and Frederick met the French king, Louis VII, another of Alexander's most dedicated supporters, in February 1171. But the emperor's policy was inconsistent – while seeking an end to the schism, he was still reluctant to acknowledge Alexander in person or to renounce the right that he had earlier claimed to intervene in Church affairs. Also, the status of those prelates who had been appointed since 1160 and received confirmation from the antipopes remained in dispute. Alexander insisted throughout that Frederick must make a personal submission to him, and publicly acknowledge him as the only legitimate pope. He was also reluctant to make any peace with Frederick that did not include his north Italian allies, whereas the emperor wanted to treat the Lombard League as an entirely separate issue, which pertained to him as emperor and had nothing to do with the pope. The negotiations therefore had no chance of success.

Frederick issued a summons for a new expedition to Italy at a diet held at Worms in March 1172. That this took two and a half years to set in motion may well reflect the lack of enthusiasm for further Italian adventures in Germany, as well as the practical difficulties of raising money and recruiting allies in northern Italy, and perhaps as well continuing hopes for some sort of diplomatic solution. By now Frederick was also trying to encourage splits in the coalition supporting the pope. A proposal was made to Manuel Komnenos that his daughter should marry the emperor's son – probably his eldest surviving son, Henry. Given that she was about twenty, and Henry six or seven, that was never a very feasible union, and anyway Manuel's terms for such a marriage would probably have been far more than Frederick would have been willing to concede, not least territorial concessions in Italy. Another proposal was sent to King William II of Sicily that he should marry the emperor's daughter – presumably in the hope of, at the very least, ensuring his neutrality. The king, however, refused and immediately reported the offer to Pope Alexander. By such a proposal Frederick was now ready to recognize the legitimacy of the Kingdom of Sicily, but he seems still to have been unable to overcome his personal antipathy to the pope, which may well have gone back to the latter's 'provocation' at the diet of Besançon in 1157, or to make concessions that seemed to him embarrassing or dishonourable.

The imperial army that entered Italy from Burgundy via the Mont Cenis pass in September 1174 numbered about 8,000.[21]

Many of these were mercenaries. The emperor was accompanied by the archbishops of Cologne and Trier, six other bishops, his half-brother Conrad, Otto of Wittelsbach, and the margraves of Vohburg and Istria (from a Bavarian comital family), but only five other German counts. Although not negligible, this army was hardly large enough to defeat the combined forces of the Lombard cities, and this raises the question of what Frederick hoped to achieve. Alexander III's biographer suggested that the emperor undertook this expedition at the request of William of Montferrat and the city of Pavia, and it may be that a desire not to abandon his few remaining local allies did influence Frederick.[22] He may also have hoped that the conflicting interests of the different cities might harm the hitherto impressive unity of the league. In addition, he seems to have been determined to destroy the new city of Alessandria, although the strategic and political benefits of doing this were limited. His motives here may have been no more than to wipe out what he considered to be a deliberate insult to him, by christening the city with the name of his hated adversary. If so, this shows once again how far Frederick allowed concern for his *amour propre* to work against his best interests. In the event, his four-month siege of Alessandria was an embarrassing failure. On Easter Sunday 1175 he withdrew before a relieving army from the league could arrive. It was probably fortunate that the Lombards still retained a healthy respect for the fighting qualities of the Germans, and a few days later, at their suggestion, peace talks began at Montebello, in the territory of Pavia. According to the admittedly hostile testimony of Cardinal Boso, Frederick had to be persuaded by his own men, and very reluctantly, to sanction these.[23] The talks, however, initially proved promising, and the Lombards willing to submit to the emperor, albeit on negotiated terms. Frederick was sufficiently encouraged to disband most of his army – the German bishops went home, and he was probably running short of money to pay his mercenaries.

Although the peace talks continued for some weeks, they ultimately failed. The Lombards were willing to make some concessions, such as paying the *fodrum* when future emperors went to Rome for their imperial coronation, but not enough to satisfy Frederick, who still hankered after the full exercise of imperial rights as laid out in the Roncaglia decrees in 1158. Furthermore, the league's negotiators insisted that peace with the Church had to be part of any agreement, and although Pope Alexander sent three cardinals to join the conference the emperor still refused, as he saw it, to capitulate to the pope's demands. Hostilities were not immediately resumed. The consuls of Cremona acted as go-betweens to continue negotiations between Frederick and the other cities – the imperial forces were too weak, and the Lombards had probably little wish, to resume full-scale warfare. But eventually the emperor sent the Archbishop of Cologne back to Germany to summon reinforcements, in the expectation that when they arrived he would make one further effort to secure victory. By the spring of 1176 he had been joined by Archbishop Wichmann of Magdeburg, six other bishops, his nephew Landgrave Ludwig (III) of Thuringia, Margrave Dietrich of Landsberg (one of the Wettin clan), the counts of Flanders and Holland, and Count Bernhard of Anhalt from Saxony. In all they had brought about 2,000 knights. In addition Frederick had been strengthened by the return to his side of Cremona and Como, both more worried by the renewed power of Milan than by the emperor. More surprisingly, Tortona, the city which Frederick had destroyed in 1155, also joined him, in return for the confirmation of its territory and privileges, and the emperor's pledge not to levy any more dues from the city than he did from Pavia, his most faithful ally.[24] There was, however, one very important absentee from this army. Frederick had requested Henry the Lion for assistance – and some accounts suggest they had met at Chiavenna in the Alps early in 1176, where Frederick had

begged the duke for his help. But Henry had refused, although
several Saxon bishops did come to join the emperor.

   Strengthened by these reinforcements, the emperor invaded
Milanese territory and on 29 May 1176 engaged the league army
in the one and only pitched battle of his wars in Italy, at Legnano
northwest of Milan. Neither side was at full strength. Frederick's
forces had spread out to ravage the Milanese *contado*, and only
about 1,000 of his German knights were with him. The core of
the league army was from Milan and five other cities – Piacenza
had sent, for example, three hundred knights – but they were
unwilling to wait for some of their infantry and contingents from
their allies to arrive. After some sharp fighting, during which the
troops from Brescia and some others of the league army fled,
Frederick's standard-bearer was killed and (according to Cardinal
Boso) the emperor himself was unhorsed. His demoralized army
fled, apart from the infantry from Como, almost all of whom were
killed or captured. Some of the German troops were drowned
in the river Ticino as they fled. The Count of Flanders and the
Margrave of Istria were captured. For some time, indeed, Frederick
was believed to have been killed – Boso said that the empress
had gone into mourning before her husband turned up at Pavia
with only a handful of attendants.[25]

   Militarily, the Battle of Legnano was a severe setback. Politically, it was a disaster. It was obvious that Frederick no longer had
the power to overcome the Lombard cities, who in turn were
much more confident after their success. It also finally convinced
Frederick that he must cut his losses and make peace. Once again
the Cremonesi acted as mediators between him and the league
– perhaps to save the emperor's honour by avoiding his making
a direct plea for peace – and a draft agreement was drawn up in
June or July 1176, in which Frederick accepted the terms that
the Lombard cities had demanded at Montebello a year earlier.[26]
An immediate truce was declared until a final settlement could

be made. Frederick also decided to make peace with the papacy and finally to recognize Alexander III as the true pope. An embassy was sent to him, headed by Archbishop Wichmann, and a draft treaty was drawn up at Anagni, south of Rome, in November, in which it was agreed in Frederick's name that there would be a 'true peace' between papacy and the empire. The emperor was to recognize the pope as the ruler of Rome and of the lands of Countess Matilda, and to return all other papal property and rights that had been confiscated during the schism. Any disputes about the details of this would be subject to arbitration. Frederick also agreed to make peace with the Lombards, the king of Sicily and the Greek emperor.[27]

Yet despite these promising beginnings, it still took another nine months for peace finally to be concluded, and for Frederick and Pope Alexander actually to meet. Long negotiations were needed to decide on a venue for, and on the procedure to be followed at, a full-scale peace conference. It is clear that the various parties did not trust each other. The emperor's diplomacy remained extremely devious, and there were frequent accusations of bad faith. The Lombards accused Frederick of wanting to conclude a separate peace with them, without making peace with the Church. Welf VI, by now firmly committed to Pope Alexander, wrote to one of the latter's cardinals in October 1176 – presumably as the emperor's envoys were on the way to Anagni – to say that Frederick still wanted to hold a council that would decide between the two popes.[28] It was agreed that the proposed conference should be held at Bologna; then the emperor claimed that this was impossible because the inhabitants of that city hated his chief negotiator, Archbishop Christian of Mainz. When the pope agreed that the conference could instead be held at Venice, the Lombards objected since they felt that the Venetians, who had originally supported the league, were now too friendly towards the emperor. Pope Alexander, who was clearly afraid that the emperor might try to seize him by force, was insistent that Frederick could not come to Venice until an agreement in principle had been concluded, and while the emperor waited at Chioggia, only a few miles away on the mainland, a plot emerged among the Venetian commoners to invite him to enter the city without permission. The Sicilian envoys responded by offering their galleys to evacuate the pope. The doge of Venice, Sebastiano Ziani, persuaded the common people to remain calm and not to break his sworn word to ensure the pope's safety, but then offended the Sicilian delegation, who threatened to withdraw. Their hurt feelings had to be soothed by the pope. At one point Frederick lost his temper with his own envoys, snarling that Archbishop Christian – his loyal supporter for many years – was more concerned with the pope's interests than with his. Christian then told Pope Alexander that he was afraid that if the preliminary negotiations were prolonged much more the emperor would become so bored that he would abandon them. It may be here that the emperor and archbishop were playing a very subtle game, in the hope of persuading the pope to make concessions. But if these stories can be taken at face value, they throw a revealing light on the emperor's character and on his continued obstinacy and wish to delay the inevitable.

If the emperor was still only a reluctant participant, the main influence which in the end forced him to settle was the German bishops, who realized, probably far more clearly than he did, that the schism had to end.[29] But the process by which it did conclude was long and involved. Pope Alexander came to Venice on 23 March 1177. The final draft of the treaty was only agreed on 22 July, and two days later Frederick arrived in Venice to be formally absolved from excommunication, and only after this was he permitted to meet the pope. Even then, there was almost a hitch. As Frederick prostrated himself as a repentant sinner before the pontiff, as protocol required, one of the German nobles watching objected loudly that this abasement was humiliating to the empire. When this was translated to the pope, he quickly helped the emperor to rise and gave him the formal kiss of peace, and the incident passed.[30] Thereafter both emperor and pope did their best to behave courteously and agreeably to each other over several weeks of further discussion.[31]

The terms of the final agreement were about as favourable as could be expected for the emperor – given that he had to submit to the pope whom he had opposed for the previous seventeen years. The issue of the lands of Countess Matilda was, for example, quietly dropped. Some pragmatic arrangements were made concerning prelates who had been appointed during the schism and consecrated by other schismatic bishops. Archbishops Philip of Cologne and Christian of Mainz, who came into this category, kept their jobs, although it was agreed that the latter's predecessor, Conrad of Wittelsbach, who had been deposed after defecting to Alexander, would be appointed to the archbishopric of Salzburg, currently in dispute. Although no final agreement was made either with the Lombards or with the king of Sicily, long truces were concluded, for six years with the former and fifteen years with the latter. In the case of the Lombards hard bargaining was still going to be needed to settle the details of a permanent peace, but for all practical purposes Frederick had recognized the legitimacy of the Lombard League and the right of the cities to govern themselves. Similarly, he had for the first time formally recognized the legitimacy of the Kingdom of Sicily. (The Byzantine emperor was not represented at the conference and was quietly forgotten.)

The Venice peace conference saw the unravelling of just about everything that Frederick had been trying to achieve in Italy over the previous twenty years. In retrospect, there had been very little prospect of his policy succeeding since the disasters of 1167. His attempt to impose his own solution to the

papal schism, and to claim that he was entitled to do this, had
failed completely, and greatly complicated his attempts to enforce his direct rule over northern Italy. If there had been at
least some support for Victor IV, if only within the empire and
nowhere else in Christendom, there had been less for Paschal
III, and very little indeed for the last antipope, Calixtus III. By
the early 1170s Frederick's own churchmen were trying to find
a way out. His obstinate refusal to recognize Alexander III long
after it was clear that the latter had 'won' the schism was a major
political drawback. Furthermore, for all his alleged intransigence
at Besançon in 1157, Alexander as pope had shown himself
surprisingly flexible towards the European monarchs, and while
not compromising the papacy's fundamental rights he had been
willing to negotiate a peace with the emperor from at least 1169
onwards. It was Frederick who had prevented such a rapprochement. Meanwhile, after the destruction of Milan in 1162 he had
seemed to be on the verge of success in northern Italy, but his
attempt to exploit his regalian rights as far as he could, and the
excesses and greed of his own officers, had undone his military
victories and alienated many of his own local allies. That cities
like Bergamo, Cremona and Lodi, which had hitherto supported
him, had joined the league was telling. His refusal to address the
grievances of the Lombards in 1166 had been a serious error.

But one might also question whether the attempt to overcome the Lombard cities through large-scale military campaigns
was really feasible. The 1158–62 campaign had certainly been
impressive, but even then very few of those who were initially
involved had lasted through to the end of the campaign. Many
of those who came to Italy stayed only a few months before seeking to return home. Admittedly, the scale of military resources
in Germany and the loyalty of German churchmen and nobles
meant that reinforcements were available, and service was provided as a sort of shuttle system. But at times he was primarily

dependent on his Italian allies, and after 1167 he had far fewer of these. Furthermore, none of his later expeditions were on the scale of 1158. During his fifth expedition of 1174–8 he was dependent on the bishops, and on a handful of nobles, most of whom were closely connected to him: relations like his half-brother Conrad and his nephew Ludwig, or long-term loyalists and friends like Otto of Wittelsbach and Count Henry of Dietz, of whom the last-named played a significant role in the negotiations leading up to the treaty of Venice, and often swore oaths in the emperor's name. Even here, while Conrad and Otto, both of whom had played a prominent part in earlier expeditions, entered Italy with him in 1174, both had returned home before the Battle of Legnano. By May 1176 his army was perhaps half the size of the one with which he had entered Italy eighteen months earlier. There seems indeed to have been an increasing lack of enthusiasm for participation in these Italian expeditions. This was not necessarily through lack of loyalty, or from opposition to the emperor's policy, although the frightful death toll from the epidemic at Rome in 1167 must have been discouraging. But it may well also have reflected the strain that such operations put on the resources of those involved, especially if they remained south of the Alps for a considerable period. Archbishop Rainald's contingent in the army of 1167 was much smaller than the one he had brought to Italy six years earlier. We have some indications of the financial strain that service in Italy imposed on the bishops. The Bishop of Halberstadt, for example, was preparing to take part in the fourth Italian expedition, and to fund this he mortgaged some of his see's property to a local abbey in November 1165 in return for 200 marks. Significantly, he noted that his predecessors had been lax in providing such service to the empire, and hence the emperor's favour had been withdrawn – it was necessary to regain this. A decade later, in 1175, Frederick ordered the cathedral chapter of Würzburg to loan its bishop

350 marks for the expenses of his participation among the reinforcements about to set off for Italy, and a year after that the
Archbishop of Cologne mortgaged two of his estates for 400
marks for the same reason. And according to his successor at
Mainz, Archbishop Christian, who was in Italy continuously from
1171 until his death in 1183, had mortgaged most of the see's
property and effectively bankrupted it.[32] Laymen no doubt faced
similar problems, particularly those like Otto of Wittelsbach
who took part in several expeditions. While participation varied
from one expedition to another, Barbarossa's regular campaigns
in Italy imposed a considerable strain on the German upper class,
and his absences from Germany, as we shall see, also created or
exacerbated political problems there.

FOUR

Germany, 1158–78

Frederick returned to the Reich via Burgundy in the summer of 1178 after lingering for some months following the Venice conference in Romagna and Tuscany, trying to bolster imperial rule in these regions to compensate for the surrender of his authority in Lombardy. For the previous twenty years Italy had been Frederick's primary concern. This did not mean, of course, that he could entirely neglect affairs in Germany, nor was he always absent from the Reich, most notably between 1168 and 1174. But his policy in Germany during these twenty years was largely subordinated to his preoccupation with reimposing imperial rule in Italy.

There were three main strands to this policy. First, and most importantly, Frederick wanted to keep Germany peaceful by avoiding rifts among the princes and great nobles and pacifying disputes that had emerged. He himself needed good relations with these major figures and to avoid distracting local squabbles so that when required they would be able and willing to take part in his Italian expeditions. It was also important that those serving in Italy did not find themselves alongside those to whom they were hostile. It may not be coincidental that after the dispute concerning Bavaria at the beginning of the reign, in 1158 Henry of Babenberg took part in the early stages of the second Italian expedition, while Henry the Lion did not and only joined the emperor in Lombardy in 1161, after the Duke of Austria had returned home. Furthermore, a major breakdown in the political consensus and in law and order in Germany would have made prolonged absence by the emperor in Italy extremely difficult. Second, he needed to retain the loyalty of the German bishops and other major churchmen. This was important for the general political stability of the kingdom, given the wealth and power of many prelates. As we have seen, bishops and their military followings also played a major part in all of his Italian expeditions, and indeed as time went on probably played a proportionally greater role than did the lay princes and nobility. There were at least as many bishops as counts with Frederick in Italy from 1174 to 1178. But control over the Church became especially significant after the papal schism in 1159–60. Having committed himself and the empire to the cause of Victor IV, at a council attended by a dozen German bishops and three from Burgundy, Frederick needed the leaders of the German Church to remain solidly behind *his* pope if the latter was to have any credibility, and particularly so since almost all the rest of Christendom soon recognized Alexander III. Third, Frederick was concerned to build up his lands and rights within Germany, both imperial property and, more importantly, that of his own family. Territorial power was still the principal basis for effective rule, and the family wealth and power of the Staufer needed augmentation if they were to retain the kingship in generations to come. This issue came to the fore after Frederick started to have children – he needed to provide for his growing brood of sons.

Since medieval rulership was intensely personal, and even more so in Germany where institutional structures for royal government, as opposed to the administration of the king/emperor's own lands, were lacking, prolonged absences by the monarch tended to be destabilizing. When Frederick returned from his first expedition to Italy in the autumn of 1155 he had been forced to deal with the conflict in the Rhineland between the

Count Palatine Hermann and Archbishop Arnold of Mainz. Here he seems to have held both parties equally at fault. During his brief period in Germany in 1162–3 he had, very belatedly, taken action to punish the citizens of Mainz for the murder of Archbishop Arnold in the summer of 1160 – the city's walls were demolished, its privileges withdrawn and some of the ringleaders exiled. This clearly was an incident of civil disorder and social upheaval so serious that Frederick could not ignore it, but he had been powerless to impose immediate punishment since he was on the other side of the Alps. More frequently, the emperor was called upon to arbitrate between competing parties and usually ended up favouring one side, although preferably without entirely alienating the other one. Such was the case with a very dangerous feud that broke out in Swabia while the emperor was in Italy in 1164. The dispute stemmed from an act of summary justice by Count Hugo of Tübingen. The sources vary as to the precise details, but he had either one or perhaps several *ministeriales* of Welf VI hanged, apparently as bandits – which the contemporary 'History of the Welfs' condemned as an unjust judgement. Another version said that he arrested three *ministeriales*, two of whom were his own men and one belonged to Welf; he pardoned his own knights but hanged the one belonging to the duke, and it was this act of blatant partiality that angered the latter. Welf tried to resolve the issue by legal measures, and at first the count appeared ready to acknowledge his fault. But after the duke had gone with the emperor to Italy in autumn 1163, leaving his son in charge of his German lands, the latter raised the case once again, and the legal dispute escalated into a full-scale military confrontation in which both sides sought allies. The Count of Tübingen relied on the backing of King Conrad's son Frederick of Rothenburg, Duke of Swabia – who was now about twenty. Welf VII mustered a coalition involving three Swabian bishops, the Duke of

Zähringen, the latter's cousin the Margrave of Baden and several local counts with an army of over 2,000 knights. Despite this imposing force, they were defeated in a pitched battle in September 1164 and a substantial part of their army was taken prisoner. Frederick returned from Italy a month later and hastened to Swabia, where he held a court at Ulm in November that imposed a one-year truce on the combatants. The truce held, but the feud remained unsettled, and Count Hugo renewed the conflict early in 1166, with the assistance of Bohemian mercenaries who caused widespread destruction. Frederick then convened a further court at Ulm in March 1166 which found in favour of Welf vi. Hugo was not only forced to submit but was handed over to the duke to be imprisoned in one of his castles and was only released eighteen months later.[1] While the count would seem to have offended the emperor by restarting a dispute in which he had personally intervened to sedate it, there were also political considerations at work. Frederick was soon to leave for Italy once again and could not afford to leave part of his kingdom, and one in which he had had many of his own lands, at war. Welf vi not only was his uncle, but had been a close ally of his since before he had become king, had been one of those who elected him in 1152 and had served in his army in Italy in 1161–2 and 1163–4. He regularly attended his court, witnessing almost a third of his charters in the first fifteen years of his reign. His son Welf vii was preparing to lead a contingent on the forthcoming Italian expedition, while his father went on pilgrimage to Jerusalem. Frederick therefore had to repay his loyalty by supporting him. But he also needed not to offend Count Hugo's principal supporter in the earlier stages of the dispute, Frederick of Rothenburg. Not only was he the titular Duke of Swabia and the emperor's first cousin, but he had brought six hundred knights to reinforce the army in Italy in 1161 and was another preparing to return to Italy in the autumn of 1166.

So while Hugo was punished, Frederick's role was discreetly ignored.

Although the Tübingen feud was perhaps the most serious, it was only one of several disputes in which the emperor intervened during his stay in Germany from 1164 to 1166. Indeed, as soon as he returned from Italy in November 1164, he had to arbitrate in a conflict about the Rhineland castle of Rheineck between his half-brother, the Count Palatine Conrad, and his trusted counsellor Rainald of Dassel – who had been sending instructions from Italy ordering his troops to oppose the count. A year later Frederick went to Utrecht to mediate in a dispute between the bishop and Count Florenz of Holland over the County of Friesland, the last incumbent of which had recently died without heir. Here he arranged a compromise: Count Florenz received the right to administer justice in Friesland, but its lands and income were otherwise to be shared between them. And in February 1166 he heard a complaint from his long-standing adviser Bishop Eberhard of Bamberg that the Duke of Carinthia had illegally seized property of his see.[2] These last two cases were very much the normal business of government in Germany – arbitrating between his great men and their conflicting claims was one of the principal tasks of the ruler. But he could only do this effectively while he was present in Germany, and if such disputes were left unresolved then they could flare up into serious fighting, as happened in the Tübingen and Rheineck cases.

An even more dangerous example of such a dispute arose in northeastern Germany while Frederick was absent on his fourth Italian expedition. The contemporary chronicler of that region, Helmold of Bosau, ascribed this to envy aroused by the wealth and success of Henry the Lion – 'all the princes of Saxony were jealous of the glory of this great man' – but claimed that these magnates had been restrained by their fear of the emperor, until the latter departed once again for Italy, leaving the field clear for

them once again to attack the duke.[3] It seems that Frederick had
forestalled an earlier alliance against the duke at a diet held at
Nuremberg in August 1163, shortly before his departure on his
fourth Italian expedition.[4] But once he departed for Italy in 1166,
for what was clearly going to be quite a long absence, the duke's
enemies saw their opportunity. The coalition against Henry in
1166 included Margrave Albrecht 'the Bear' of Brandenburg,
Margrave Otto of Meissen and the rest of the Wettin clan, the
Landgrave of Thuringia, the counts palatine of Sommerschenburg,
Count Christian of Oldenburg, the archbishops of Magdeburg
and (somewhat belatedly) Bremen, and the Bishop of Hildesheim
– in other words almost all the princes and several other major
nobles from northeast Germany. Some of these men had long-
standing grievances against Henry the Lion and his family. In
particular Albrecht the Bear and his family (often known as the
Ascanians) had always resented that the Welfs had received the
lion's share of the inheritance of the Billung family, the former
dukes of Saxony, the last of whom, Magnus, had died in 1106.
Both Henry the Lion and Albrecht were descended from daughters of Duke Magnus, but the resulting share-out of the duke's
property had been far from equal. Furthermore, Conrad III had,
soon after his accession, appointed Albrecht as Duke of Saxony
but had eventually been forced to recognize the claim of the
young Henry the Lion in 1142. Albrecht had little choice but to
acquiesce in his loss of status but can hardly have been happy
about this.

Similarly, Archbishop Hartwig of Bremen resented not only
Henry's overbearing behaviour as advocate of the see and his
effective control of several bishoprics that were ecclesiastically
subordinate to Bremen, but more particularly his seizure of the
County of Stade after the death of the last count in 1144 – for
Hartwig himself was the last male member of that family and had
wanted to add the county to the endowment of his archbishopric.

Ever since attaining his majority, Henry had displayed both abundant energy and a lack of scruple in extending his property and rights and consolidating his position as the dominant power in eastern Saxony. The retention of the County of Stade, his annexation of the new and potentially profitable trading port of Lübeck from Count Adolf of Holstein circa 1158 and his attempts to draw the *ministeriales* of the Bishop of Hildesheim into his own following were cases in point. Similarly, his efforts to extend his lands south of the Harz mountains had brought him into conflict with the Landgrave of Thuringia. In expanding his lands and fiscal and judicial rights the duke was doing nothing very different from what his neighbours and competitors were also doing – but he was doing this on a much larger scale with a cavalier disregard for the claims of others, and so the dislike he aroused is entirely understandable.

While the emperor was in Italy this festering resentment broke out into open warfare. Early in 1167 the duke captured and sacked Bremen, and after a long siege also captured Oldenburg,

THE BILLUNG INHERITANCE

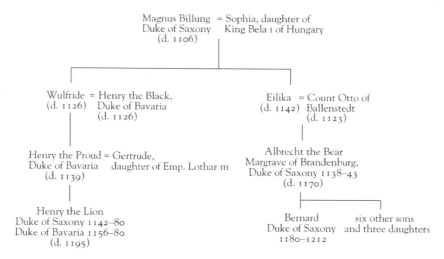

Magnus Billung = Sophia, daughter of
Duke of Saxony   King Bela I of Hungary
(d. 1106)

Wulfride = Henry the Black,
(d. 1126)   Duke of Bavaria
(d. 1126)

Henry the Proud = Gertrude,
Duke of Bavaria   daughter of Emp. Lothar III
(d. 1139)

Henry the Lion
Duke of Saxony 1142–80
Duke of Bavaria 1156–80
(d. 1195)

Eilika   = Count Otto of
(d. 1142)   Ballenstedt
(d. 1123)

Albrecht the Bear
Margrave of Brandenburg,
Duke of Saxony 1138–43
(d. 1170)

Bernard   six other sons
Duke of Saxony   and three daughters
1180–1212

which he added to his lands. Meanwhile his enemies captured Goslar (an imperial town, but around which the duke had extensive property), in retaliation for which Henry ravaged the diocese of Hildesheim. Then, after the death of Archbishop Hartwig in October 1168, both sides sought to impose their own candidate as the next archbishop, and this led to a fresh outbreak of violence. Various orders sent by the emperor from Italy for the combatants to cease hostilities were ignored.

There can be no doubt that Frederick and Henry had been close in the early years of the reign. Henry was, after all, the emperor's cousin, had played a key part in his election and during the first ten years of the reign had regularly been at court, witnessing almost two-thirds of the charters issued in Frederick's name in Germany, more than anyone else. He had also taken part in the first two Italian expeditions and Frederick had reinstated him, not without difficulty, as Duke of Bavaria. Admittedly after 1162 there was less frequent contact, but in the twelve years up to 1174 he still witnessed about a fifth of the emperor's charters and was present at important meetings such as the settlement of the Tübingen feud at Ulm in March 1166. Other signs of how closely the two were allied in the early years of the reign were Frederick's grant of delegated imperial authority over the three new bishoprics along the Saxon–Slav frontier in 1154, and then a large-scale exchange of property between the two at Goslar on 1 January 1158, with Henry giving the emperor land and *ministeriales* in Swabia, in return for lands and castles in the Harz region of Saxony.[5] This exchange enabled both men to strengthen their power base in key areas for their rule. It was hardly surprising, therefore, that when Frederick eventually returned to Germany in 1168, he took the duke's side, as he had done earlier. He went to Saxony in person early in 1169, instructed everyone to keep the peace and took hostages from some of Henry's opponents. Then, at a diet held at Bamberg in

June 1169 he brokered a comprehensive peace deal, but even this apparent settlement did not solve all the problems and once again Frederick had to go to Saxony. Finally, he brought about a more lasting agreement at Erfurt in June 1170, very much in Henry's favour. The duke kept most of his acquisitions, and after quashing the election of both candidates at Bremen the emperor imposed his own nominee as archbishop, who was a close ally of the duke. Soon afterwards the death of Albrecht the Bear removed Henry's most bitter and dangerous rival.

For Frederick, ending what was in effect a civil war in north-east Germany was necessary both for his own prestige as ruler and to ensure that the kingdom remained stable should he undertake another Italian expedition – which of course he did in 1174. Keeping the peace and resolving disputes among the princes was his most important governmental task within the Reich, and the perception that he would be able to do this effectively had played a significant part in the acquiescence of the princes to his usurpation of the throne in 1152. And despite the recent disaster in Italy his ability to enforce a peace settlement, while clearly by no means easy, suggests that his authority as ruler of Germany was still strong. What the sources do not, however, reveal is exactly how Henry the Lion's opponents were induced to abandon their struggle, and what if anything the emperor may have done to pacify them. For while Duke Henry was the emperor's relative and still his ally, to whom he was politically indebted, Frederick also had close ties to some of his opponents. Landgrave Ludwig (II) of Thuringia was his brother-in-law. He had also taken part in the second and fourth Italian expeditions. Margrave Otto of Meissen and two of his brothers had taken part in the 1158 and 1163 expeditions, and two other brothers in the most recent, 1166–8, campaign. Archbishop Wichmann of Magdeburg, whose mother was a Wettin, had been Frederick's own nominee for this see, had served the emperor loyally and regularly attended his court. Frederick was not, therefore, in a position simply to browbeat these men into submission, even if he had had the power to do so – which is doubtful. Some quite delicate persuasion must have been involved. But, once again, it was the emperor's presence that was effective in restoring peace and order. While the tensions between Duke Henry and his opponents remained, they were not to flare up again into open conflict for some years, and the situation in Saxony was sufficiently peaceful to allow the duke to go on pilgrimage to Jerusalem in 1172, a journey which caused him to be away from Germany for almost a year – without his enemies taking advantage of his absence – although this was at a time when the emperor was still present in the Reich. Yet if Saxony was at peace in the early 1170s, local tensions in other regions still required the emperor's attention. Shortly before his departure to Italy in 1174 he had sharply to order Duke Hermann of Carinthia to cease a feud he had commenced with the Margrave of Styria until the two could appear before him to resolve their differences.[6] Keeping the peace between the great men of the kingdom was a continuing process.

The second strand to Frederick's policy in Germany was his relations with the leaders of the Church. Given the wealth and power of the Church this was always important, but the papal schism made it all the more so. With most of Christendom siding with Alexander, Frederick needed the Church in his power base to remain loyal to Victor IV and his successors if the latter were to have any chance of ultimately prevailing. For the most part, and for a considerable period, he was surprisingly successful in this aim, although after 1168, in particular, many of the German prelates would probably have preferred to find a solution to the schism, which would inevitably have involved accepting Alexander as the legitimate pope rather than the obscure Calixtus III, who was personally unknown both to the emperor and to nearly all of his bishops. But even then loyalty to Frederick stopped them breaking ranks, at least overtly.

Two factors, in particular, contributed to this loyalty. While after the concordat of 1122 the right of cathedral chapters as the electing body for bishops was acknowledged, in practice the emperor was often involved in these elections and sometimes had the decisive say in choosing who was to be appointed, especially if the chapter was unable to agree on a candidate – a not at all unusual occurrence. A prime example was the choice of Wichmann as Archbishop of Magdeburg, right at the start of the reign. Here the issue had been complicated because Wichmann was already a bishop of another Saxon see, Zeitz, and had been since 1149, and canon law was clear that the translation of a bishop from one see to another needed papal permission, which in this case was granted only reluctantly. But here Frederick was able to set aside both the original candidates and impose his own man and persuade the pope to ratify his choice in 1154. His success in securing bishoprics for his own clerical administrators was also notable. Successive royal chancellors were chosen as prelates of important German sees: Rainald of Dassel as Archbishop of Cologne in 1159; Ulrich of Dürrmenz as Bishop of Speyer in 1161; Christian of Buch, chancellor and Frederick's legate in Italy, elected Archbishop of Mainz in 1165; and Philip of Heinsberg as Archbishop of Cologne in 1167. Furthermore, all four of these were elected while they were absent in Italy. In all these cases the emperor's voice was decisive; in that of Philip we have unequivocal evidence for Frederick's intervention, for his letter to the provost (the head of the chapter) at Cologne, written from outside Rome in August 1167, survives. Frederick notified him of Archbishop Rainald's death and then recommended his chancellor, Philip, whom he said was outstanding in his 'administration of the empire' and admirably suited for the see. He continued,

Statue of Archbishop Wichmann of Magdeburg, Magdeburg Cathedral.

For this reason we seek with all our heart that he be
chosen as we desire, so that your diligence in effecting
his promotion will provide strong reasons for our favour
and for the reception of rich rewards in the future.[7]

The chapter duly took this far from subtle hint and elected
the chancellor. Similarly, a month later the emperor wrote both
to the cathedral chapter and to Count Thierry of Flanders and
his son Philip concerning the choice of a new bishop of Cambrai
– a see where he had had some difficulties with the previous
bishop, Nicholas, who had also been at odds with the count.
Here too the chapter had failed to agree on a candidate to replace
the deceased prelate. In his letter to the counts Frederick proclaimed high-mindedly that 'we have always preserved the
freedom of election unimpaired,' but at the same time he said
that he was sending envoys to ensure the unanimous election
of 'a suitable person for God and the empire', while in his letter
to the chapter he made clear that if they could not agree on a
candidate he would simply appoint one, as indeed he was entitled to do under the terms of the 1122 concordat.[8] The chapter
then elected the candidate favoured by Frederick's ally the count.
(That Count Thierry was a relation of the empress doubtless
also helped his cause.) Other elections followed the same pattern, such as that of Archbishop Arnold of Trier in 1169, which
the contemporary historian of that see admitted was 'on the suggestion and advice of the emperor', and took place even though
Arnold was at that point a stranger to the chapter.[9] Such imperial
intervention was not universal, particularly in the more periph-
eral sees in the kingdom, but it *was* frequent, especially with
regard to the archbishoprics and some of the wealthier sees in
central and southern Germany. Although there are quite a number of cases where we have no information, it has been calculated
that, over the reign as a whole, Frederick exercised at least some

influence over the choice of about a third of all the bishops elected in Germany.

The second factor involved was the social background of the episcopate. The higher ranks of the German clergy, both bishops and the cathedral chapters by whom they were elected (as well as most abbots of monasteries), were overwhelmingly aristocrats, often the younger brothers or sons of counts and sometimes of princes. The German aristocracy remained conspicuously loyal to Frederick, even if their enthusiasm for adventures in Italy may have waned as time went by. This was a strong incentive for the prelates who were related to them also to stay loyal, although the wish to conciliate particular families, as well as their often overwhelming local influence, might sometimes complicate the choice of bishops. A case in point came with the choice of a new archbishop of Mainz, to replace the murdered Archbishop Arnold. A disputed election pitted Rudolf, the younger brother of Duke Berthold (IV) of Zähringen, against Christian of Buch, who was supported by the Landgrave of Thuringia. Frederick rejected both candidates and 'persuaded' the chapter to choose Conrad, the younger brother of his close friend and ally Otto of Wittelsbach, a move that was presumably intended to bind this influential Bavarian family even more closely to him than they had been previously. But it led to the Zähringen family becoming estranged from the emperor for several years, although after the duke had taken part in the Italian expedition of 1166 his brother Rudolf was compensated with the bishopric of Liège in 1167. Christian of Buch, who in the meanwhile had become a key figure in the emperor's Italian campaigns, finally gained the archbishopric in 1165.

In the early stages of the schism only a few German prelates broke ranks – almost all of whom were from the metropolitan province of Salzburg in the southeast. The foremost among these was the metropolitan himself, Eberhard, who had been

Archbishop of Salzburg since 1147. Without openly defying
Frederick, Eberhard managed, on plea of illness, to avoid attending the council of Pavia that recognized Victor IV as pope, and
never did acknowledge him. He also failed to provide the military service that the emperor requested from him in Italy, despite
a series of increasingly angry reproofs and demands, and eventually threats, from the emperor. The archbishop was already in
correspondence with Alexander, who in 1163 appointed him
his legate in Germany, and one of his suffragans, Bishop Albrecht
of Freising, attended the council of Tours. That Frederick in the
end never moved openly against Eberhard may well have been
because of the latter's reputation for extraordinary piety and
goodness, to which Rahewin paid eloquent tribute.[10] Attacking
a figure of such acknowledged saintliness might well have been
counterproductive, and since Eberhard was now elderly it may
well have seemed more prudent to wait until nature took its
course. But although Eberhard died in June 1164, his successors
remained equally loyal to Alexander, and had considerable support among the clergy of the archdiocese and province, and from
the archiepiscopal *ministeriales* and people of Salzburg.

The decisive moment in the hardening of attitudes towards
the schism came with a diet held at Würzburg in May 1165.
This council, which was attended by a considerable number
of bishops, although only a few lay princes, met in theory to find
a solution to the schism. There seems to have been some initial
debate, with Archbishop Conrad of Mainz arguing for the recognition of Alexander, while Rainald of Cologne insisted on
maintaining the cause of Paschal III, recently elected to succeed
the deceased Victor IV. Rainald claimed (mendaciously) that
Henry II of England, whom he had recently met, was prepared
to follow the emperor's lead, and this was confirmed by that
king's envoy to the imperial court, John of Oxford, dean of
Salisbury. The emperor then ordered all those present to swear

that they would never recognize the 'schismatic' Rolando (Alexander III) as pope, and he himself publicly swore that he would never do so – contrary to the tradition that emperors did not swear oaths in person but instead had subordinates do this on their behalf. At least some of the prelates took this oath reluctantly – Archbishop Wichmann of Magdeburg apparently in tears and saying that he would prefer to relinquish the temporalities of his see held from the emperor – but swear they did, with one conspicuous exception. Conrad of Mainz left the council, abandoned his see and fled to join Pope Alexander in France. The emperor promptly declared the see of Mainz vacant and engineered the election of his chancellor, Christian of Buch, as the new archbishop. Over the next few months those bishops who for whatever reason had not attended the council were persuaded or coerced into swearing the oath and making the clergy in their diocese swear this too. Those who did so included even Albrecht of Freising, previously an overt supporter of Alexander.

The diet of Würzburg showed Frederick's determination not to accept Alexander as pope and made securing a solution to the schism even more difficult, not least because the emperor could now hardly change his policy without considerable loss of face. It also led to a hardening of measures against those prominent supporters of Alexander who remained recalcitrant. Conrad of Mainz was deposed, and in 1166 Frederick declared the new Archbishop of Salzburg, another Conrad, to be an outlaw and encouraged his neighbours to attack the possessions of that see, despite Conrad being the younger brother of the Duke of Austria. This relationship may have protected him against deposition, although he spent the last two years of his brief pontificate – he died in 1168 – in hiding in the Alps. But his successor Adalbert, a son of the king of Bohemia, who was also an Alexandrine supporter, *was* deposed in 1173, even though it was clear by that time that enthusiasm for the third imperial antipope, John of Struma (Calixtus III) was very limited. Where Adalbert made himself vulnerable was openly to support Alexander, whereas other prelates who were unhappy with the continuance of the schism, like Wichmann of Magdeburg, remained loyal to Frederick while working behind the scenes to try to broker a peace settlement. For, whereas there was at least a case for supporting Victor IV, it was clear by the late 1160s that the Church of Christendom overwhelmingly supported Alexander, that other monarchs were not going to follow Frederick's lead – Henry II had immediately disavowed his envoy's recognition of the antipope at the diet of Würzburg – and that there was little prospect of the emperor overcoming the north Italian cities, who had firmly committed themselves to the cause of Pope Alexander. That the schism lasted as long as it did was therefore largely due to Frederick's obstinacy, and to his fear of damaging his prestige by surrendering not just 'his' pope but also his claim that as emperor it was his right to oversee and 'protect' the papacy. In the circumstances, therefore, the loyalty of most German Church leaders to Frederick was impressive, and they played an increasingly important role in his Italian expeditions. Outside the Salzburg province, very few broke ranks. Bishop Ulrich of Halberstadt was deposed right at the start of the schism for recognizing Alexander, and Abbo of Passau in 1169 for refusing to receive consecration from his metropolitan, the intruder Christian of Buch – though Abbo also seems to have been at odds with his own clergy and the people of Passau, which doubtless made his removal easier. But, apart from innate loyalty to the emperor and the influence of their relatives, few of the worldly German episcopate wanted to forfeit the power and influence of their positions. After 1170, however, there were indications that clerical opinion within the Reich, and especially in its monasteries, was inclining towards Alexander. A number of monasteries, and not just in the province of Salzburg, sought privileges from him. The third imperial antipope, Calixtus, was largely ignored.

The third major theme of Frederick's rule in Germany was his concern to build up his own and his family's power base within the kingdom. At the start of his reign, Frederick's own landed resources were surprisingly modest, above all because it was politically necessary to provide an endowment for Frederick of Rothenburg as Duke of Swabia. While Frederick Barbarossa retained the Staufen lands in Alsace for himself, his cousin received a substantial part of the family lands in Swabia, as well as the property in Franconia that he inherited directly from his father, Conrad III. Frederick also needed to provide some endowment for his half-brother Conrad, although he largely did this through his bestowal upon him of the lands and title of the childless Count Palatine of the Rhine, Hermann of Stahleck, the husband of his maternal aunt Gertrude, who died in October 1156. Frederick did increase his landed base in Swabia through his exchange with Henry the Lion in 1158, although this was at the cost of diminishing his already relatively limited holdings in southern Saxony. The birth of his sons, the two eldest Frederick in 1164 and Henry in November 1165, with others following, meant that the issue became more pressing, since they would at some stage require their own endowments. What really changed the situation, however, was the disastrous epidemic that felled his army in Italy in 1167. First and foremost among the casualties was his cousin Frederick of Rothenburg, whose lands, including the extensive fiefs he held from a number of churches, notably the abbey of Fulda, reverted back to the emperor, and at a stroke transformed his territorial endowment within southwest Germany. In addition, a number of other lords lost their heirs and were faced with the extinction of their family in the male line. During the 1170s Frederick acquired the lands, or the expectation of succeeding to the lands, of three wealthy and important south German nobles, all of whom had lost their sons in 1167. First, there was Count Rudolf of Pfullendorf, whose lordship lay near Lake Constance and who had accompanied Frederick on crusade in 1147. Subsequently he had been his loyal supporter when he became king and emperor and had regularly attended his court, as well as taking part in the second and fourth Italian expeditions. Rudolf himself seems only to have died about 1180, while on pilgrimage to the Holy Land, but ten years earlier the fiefs that he held from the bishopric of Chur, and the right of advocacy over the bishopric, had already been assigned, with his consent, to the emperor's third son, Frederick (born 1167).[11] A dominant position in the diocese of Chur gave the emperor control over the Splügen and Septimer passes into Italy. The Pfullendorf inheritance ultimately went to the Staufer, although Rudolf had left a daughter, who was married to Count Albrecht of Habsburg. They were compensated with the county of Zurich and the advocacies of several monasteries in that region, which the emperor had acquired from another Swabian count who had died without heirs, Ulrich of Lenzburg – also a close associate of the emperor who had taken part in the first two Italian expeditions. Second, Frederick secured the reversion of the lands of the Bavarian count Gebhard of Sulzbach. While the count died considerably later, towards the end of the reign the extensive fiefs that he held in Franconia from the bishopric of Bamberg were transferred to Frederick's sons, Frederick and Otto (born 1170), in July 1174.[12] Since they were only small children, these lands, like the Pfullendorf inheritance, remained in the emperor's hands until quite late in his reign.

Third, and most important of all, Frederick consolidated his dominant position in Swabia by gaining the inheritance of Duke Welf VI. This acquisition also had significant political conse-quences. After the death of his only son in 1167, Duke Welf had

Beatrice	born 1162/3, died c. early 1174
Frederick [A]	born 18 July 1164, died summer/autumn 1169
Henry	born November 1165, died 26 September 1197
Conrad, later Frederick [B]	born February 1167, died 20 January 1191
Daughter [name unknown]	born October/November 1168, died late 1184
Otto	born June/July 1170, died 2 January 1200
Conrad [B]	born February/March 1172, died 15 August 1196
Rainald	born October/November 1173, died probably April 1174, perhaps later
William	born June/July 1175, died soon after October 1178
Philip	born February/March 1177, died 21 June 1208
Agnes	born early 1179, died 8 October 1184

Frederick Barbarossa's children. This reconstruction, based on that by Erwin Assmann, is the most probable one, but some elements, especially as regards the daughters, are conjectural.

largely withdrawn from political involvement. As the family's contemporary historian explained, he was estranged from his wife and the prospect of another heir was unlikely:

> he took pleasure rather in the embraces of others, and took pains to live the good life, spending his time in hunting, banquets and indulging in the delights of the flesh, though he appeared also generous on festival days and in making donations [to churches].[13]

This lifestyle of whoring, partying and piety proved expensive, and circa 1173 he sold his rights to his Italian lordships

Imperial Palace, Gelnhausen.

to the emperor – who in practice had long been administering these since Welf had only rarely taken an interest in them. His original intention was for his nephew in the male line, Henry the Lion, to succeed him in his south German lordships. Had this taken place it would have marked a massive accretion in the latter's power. But Welf still needed cash and sought a substantial sum of money from his nephew in return for designating him his heir. Henry the Lion, however, proved tight-fisted, reckoning, so Otto of St Blasien later suggested, that his uncle, now in his sixties, would anyway soon die.[14] This was a double miscalculation – Duke Welf actually lived to be 75, but also because, more seriously, he then turned to his other nephew, the emperor, who *was* willing to finance his uncle's expensive lifestyle in return for the succession to his lands. They came to an agreement in January 1179, with Barbarossa taking possession of some of the lands immediately, while restoring the rest to his uncle as a fief, with some other Staufen property thrown in, on condition that he and his sons would inherit all these on the duke's death. Frederick's acquisition of the succession to Duke Welf helped to sour the relationship between him and Henry the Lion, which was already becoming problematic

during the 1170s, as well as in the long run to consolidate the
Staufen hold in Swabia and to extend their lands into western
Bavaria.

These three very significant territorial acquisitions were,
however, part of a much wider policy, especially in the Duchy
of Swabia. After describing how Frederick had gained the Welf
and Pfullendorf inheritances, Otto of St Blasien continued, 'he
gained through gift or for a price the property of many other
nobles who lacked heirs', naming those of eight families known
to him from Swabia and adding that there were 'many others'
elsewhere whose names he did not know. He added that the
emperor also dispossessed the Zähringen from Burgundy, and
thereby gained the advocacies and regalian rights of the three
bishoprics of Lausanne, Geneva and Sion, and that he distributed
the fiefs that he had gained from bishops and abbots to his sons.[15]
This accumulation of land and judicial rights was not, in essence,
different from what other aspiring princely dynasties were doing
at the same time, but Frederick's acquisitions were much larger
in scale – and in Swabia, and perhaps elsewhere, he seems also
to have been reviving a royal right of claiming the property of
those who died without heir.

In addition to these extensive territorial acquisitions in south
Germany, Frederick and his servants were also active in developing his existing lands and consolidating other new power
blocs. The most significant of the latter were in the Pleissenland,
on the southeastern border of Saxony, around the castle of
Altenburg, which Frederick visited six times between 1165 and
1188, and in the Wetterau in Franconia, of which the key centre
was his new palace at Gelnhausen, where he is known to have
stayed seven times from 1170 onwards and which displaced
Frankfurt as the emperor's main base in this region. Gelnhausen
was indeed the place where Frederick promulgated one of the
most important measures of his entire reign – the confiscation

and regranting of the Duchy of Saxony in 1180. Frederick also established a 'new town' alongside the castle and palace at Gelnhausen, granting privileged status to the merchants who settled there.[16] Soon afterwards a mint was established there. Here he was developing a region where the Staufer had long had a foothold. By contrast, the Pleissenland was a frontier district where German settlers were installed in what had previously been thinly populated Slav territory. The town of Chemnitz was established here circa 1165 as a trading centre for the region. The Pleissenland was imperial rather than family territory, but almost all Frederick's other efforts to expand his landed base were intended to increase his own personal possessions or those of his sons, to cement the position of the Staufer as the wealthiest and most powerful family within Germany, to insert his sons among the imperial princes, and thus to ensure that the kingship would remain with his family. And to ensure this succession, Frederick arranged for his eldest surviving son, Henry, to be elected king in June 1169, at Bamberg – although he was at the time still only three years old.[17] But in the future, as Frederick's plans for the endowment of his sons developed, Henry would be supported by his younger brothers – Frederick as Duke of Swabia, endowed with the Welf and Pfullendorf lands; Otto as the heir to his mother in Burgundy; and Conrad, Frederick's fourth surviving son (born c. 1172) with the lands of Frederick of Rothenburg in both northern Swabia and Franconia. Thus among the twenty or so lay imperial princes, those lords directly dependent on the emperor and on nobody else, the Staufer would have four places. This would ensure their monopoly of the Crown for the foreseeable future. But in the meanwhile, until his sons were old enough to play an independent role, Frederick controlled all his vast accumulation of lands, advocacies, judicial rights, castles and *ministeriales*. The scale of this endowment by the later stages of the reign can be seen from the castles – it has been estimated that Frederick possessed perhaps two hundred of these; his nearest rival, Henry the Lion, had about fifty.

One final and very important question remains. How did Frederick actually rule Germany, and indeed in what sense did he govern it? The evidence for active government is relatively slight, and that is by no means coincidental. For much of the 1170s, for example, there appears to have been only one notary at court writing Frederick's documents, which hardly suggests an expanding bureaucracy. Insofar as we do have some evidence for an organized administration, this relates almost exclusively to the emperor's own lands. Thus while the sworn inquest into disputes and administrative problems, a key practice of other medieval governments, was sometimes used, almost all the evidence for this relates to Staufen lands and officials in Alsace, a region where the family was strongly entrenched, and had been before Frederick became king. Government within the kingdom as a whole was intensely personal, based above all on the ruler's role in settling disputes, as we have seen. Much of this was done at periodic assemblies, where the great men of the Reich gathered in the emperor's presence. So, for example, when early in 1174 Frederick sought to resolve the feud that had arisen between the Duke of Carinthia and the Margrave of Styria, he ordered the former to observe a truce until he could appear before the emperor at a diet at Regensburg, where justice would be done. But while princes and nobles might come to assemblies, and these played an important role in keeping them in touch with the emperor, there was no one set place for these, and far from remaining at a seat of government, when the emperor was in Germany he spent his time travelling round his kingdom. Indeed, if we are to measure the effectiveness of government, a key indicator is the extent of the royal itinerary. And here there was a significant change during the reign. Until 1174 Frederick traversed much of his kingdom, apart from the extreme north of Saxony, although his most frequent journeys always took place in Swabia and Franconia. But he did, for example, venture into lower Lotharingia, visiting Aachen at least six times after his coronation, Cologne eight times and Nijmegen on four known occasions – and it was in this last town that his son Henry was born in 1165. After his return from Italy in 1178 his itinerary was more restricted. He did not visit lower Lotharingia again after 1174, nor Westphalia, and his last visit to Burgundy took place during his return journey from Italy in 1178.

The extent of his travelling remained phenomenal, and Frederick must have spent much of his life in the saddle, and many of his nights in a (no doubt well-appointed) tent. King Henry II of England sent the emperor a splendid tent as a dip-lomatic gift in 1157. To illustrate how the emperor ruled we may take a single year, a not untypical one, in which he was in Germany throughout the year. At the start of 1165 Frederick travelled more than 480 kilometres (300 mi.) northeast across the kingdom from Straßburg, where he had spent Christmas, to Goslar in southern Saxony, where there was a long-established royal palace. He was at Goslar in early February, then went to Altenburg in the Pleissenland, his first known visit there, but by no means his last. He remained in south Saxony until mid-March, then headed south into Franconia. By the end of the month he was at the great imperial monastery of Fulda. By Easter (4 April) he was at Frankfurt, where he remained for two weeks, then he travelled around 130 kilometres (80 mi.) east to Würzburg, where he remained for three weeks over Whitsun, holding a diet there (where those attending had to swear to support the antipope). From Würzburg he entered Bavaria, and by the end of June he was at Passau. From there he went by boat down the Danube to Vienna, where he spent two weeks, and then he had a meeting on the Hungarian border, seeking the arrears of tribute owed by that kingdom; in August he returned

to Franconia, where he probably remained for several weeks. At
the end of September he spent at least a week at Worms, during
which time he granted an important privilege to the moneyers
of the city, then he travelled down the Rhine, probably by boat,
to Cologne, then to Nijmegen – where the empress gave birth
to their son Henry – and Utrecht, before spending Christmas

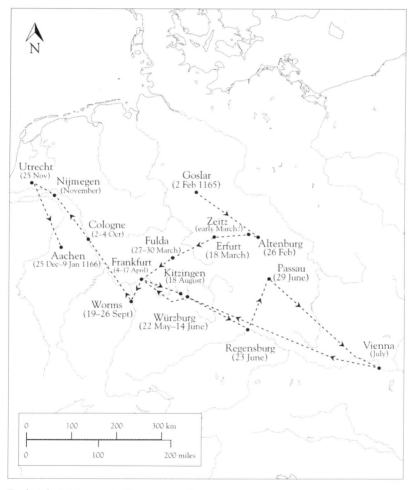

Frederick I's itinerary in Germany, 1165.

and the New Year at Aachen. By the end of January he was back
in Frankfurt. There were pauses for rest and recuperation, and
river journeys were clearly less exhausting than riding, but the
effort involved in this relentless travelling needs to be appre-
ciated. One should also remember that Frederick did not travel
alone. His chaplains accompanied him, one or more of whom
would be his notaries, as did his domestic servants, grooms and
huntsmen, and a substantial bodyguard, many of whom were
imperial *ministeriales*. The empress usually accompanied him,
with her household, until relatively late in the reign. Local magnates escorting them, and petitioners seeking help and favours
from the emperor, would have joined the entourage. We must
imagine, therefore, a cortège of several hundred people, perhaps
more, who needed to be housed, even if sometimes under can-
vas, and fed – and in the case of the emperor and his immediate
entourage, fed lavishly. To arrange all this must have required
considerable planning. Probably the only times in his life when
Frederick had but a handful of companions with him was during
his ignominious flight from Susa in 1168 and, briefly, after the
defeat at Legnano.

Two centuries earlier, the Ottonian monarchs, equally itin-
erant, had progressed around the Reich largely from one royal
estate to another, where they and their companions consumed
the food produced, and in addition often stayed at those favoured
royal monasteries which enjoyed immunity from secular jurisdiction, apart from that of the king. The corollary for a privilege
of immunity was that the abbey would be expected to entertain
the monarch and his entourage from time to time. By the
twelfth century the itinerary had altered, and not just in that
the most frequently visited region had changed from Saxony
to Franconia and Swabia. The only abbey where Frederick
stayed a number of times was Fulda. By the twelfth century few
of the other imperial abbeys now had the resources to support

such a visit. Following a pattern already established under Conrad III, roughly a third of Barbarossa's recorded stops on his travels within Germany were in episcopal cities, and he usually celebrated major church festivals, and especially Christmas, at such cities. The most frequently visited were Worms (eighteen known visits during the reign as a whole), Würzburg (seventeen), Regensburg (sixteen), Augsburg (ten) and Speyer (nine). He also made eleven stays at Erfurt, a town belonging to the Archbishop of Mainz, although only five visits are known to Mainz itself. That is explicable since that city was conspicuously out of favour after the murder of Archbishop Arnold in 1160; it was then badly damaged by a fire in 1165 and Archbishop Christian was almost always in Italy, so not in a position to play host. Three of these five visits came late in the reign, and the emperor held important assemblies there in 1184 and 1188. Frederick also made frequent visits to a small number of palace complexes, notably Goslar (eleven stays, eight of which were before 1174); Hagenau, possibly his birthplace (nine recorded visits); and to three new palaces built during the reign, Ulm, where the palace was situated in what was a reasonably flourishing town (thirteen visits), Kaiserslautern, which was next to a major royal forest and may have been a retreat for hunting, and Gelnhausen (both with seven known visits). Gelnhausen displaced nearby Frankfurt as the favourite residence in the Wetterau in western Franconia. Ulm was at the junction of several important roads and was thus a natural stopping point. Similarly, Augsburg was the departure point for four of the six expeditions to Italy. Nuremberg, which belonged to the Staufer and had a palace, inside the town, was another favoured centre which the emperor visited twelve times during his reign. Nuremberg was part of Frederick of Rothenburg's share of the Staufen lands and only passed into the emperor's hands after his death. Nevertheless, he made four visits there between 1156 and 1166. Otherwise Frederick rarely stayed with lay magnates – one of the few other times that he is known to have done so was with Otto of Wittelsbach, one of his closest friends, near Regensburg in 1156, before the diet at which the future of the Duchy of Bavaria was finally decided. Nor did he often stay at even his own castles – the palaces were probably more comfortable, and better designed for the reception of large numbers. Even Trifels in the Rheinpfalz, a long-standing possession of the Staufer around which they had a complex of lands, and which was to be much favoured by Henry vi, saw only four visits from Frederick – although its precipitous site, on a steep hill 500 metres (1,640 ft) above sea level, while admirable for defence, was hardly designed for the easy accommodation of large numbers of people.

There is much that we can only conjecture about how this royal travelling was managed, but the burden of such visits to episcopal cities must have been considerable. It was probably easier at Regensburg, where the emperor had his own palace within the city, than, for example, at Worms, where he probably stayed in the bishop's residence. Royal estates would presumably have provided food renders, as detailed in the so-called *Tafelgüterverzeichnis* at the start of the reign,[18] and probably Staufen family property too, but it is unlikely that these would have been sufficient – not least since, while the food renders listed in the schedule of royal estates provided copious quantities of meat, eggs, beer and wine, there was no mention here either of grain or of fish (the latter important in the medieval diet for religious reasons, especially in Lent). The episcopal cities were also trading centres, with markets, where purchase of other commodities would have been possible, but who paid for these? It is probable that some, perhaps most, of the costs fell on the bishop, and there are indications that this could cause problems. As one of the provisions in Frederick's privilege to the moneyers of Worms in 1165 laid down,

> If the emperor or king shall come to Worms with a great
> multitude, and it is impossible for the Bishop of Worms to
> provide for the host of *ministeriales*, then the moneyers shall
> assist to make good the place's shortfall from these *minis-
> teriales*, from the money that is in the imperial chamber.[19]

In other words, the bishop would provide for much of the emperor's following, but if his resources did not suffice, then he would
be subsidized from the emperor's own ready cash, stored in the
city. The burden would be proportionally heavier if the emperor's visit was the occasion for holding an assembly (diet), and
these were a regular occurrence – there were more than 150 held
in Germany during the course of the reign and seven in Burgundy.
Admittedly, attendance at such assemblies varied, and apart from
exceptionally important meetings was probably largely from
the province where the diet was held. But for the great assembly at Mainz in 1184, attended by virtually all the great men of
the Reich, most with a numerous following, the city itself was
too cramped to accommodate them all, and a temporary camp
was established outside, with a wooden church and palace, and
even large hen houses, 'not without wonder to many, who did
not believe that there could be so many chickens in these lands'.[20]
Most of those who attended, however, stayed in tents, which
presumably they provided themselves.

 There was no regular pattern to such travelling, and the emperor's itinerary tended to be dictated by the needs of the moment.
Hence his visits to Utrecht (one of his less frequent destinations)
took place in 1152, not just as part of his post-coronation progress but also to decide a disputed episcopal election and to quell
a revolt by the citizens, and at the end of 1165, to mediate in the
dispute between the bishop and the Count of Holland. His visit
to Vienna in that same year – the only time he went there until
the crusade at the end of his life – was because of his wish to

coerce the churchmen of the region into supporting his antipope and to further his relations with the kingdom of Hungary. This reactive element in his travelling might indeed be seen as a metaphor for his government of Germany as a whole. Frederick tended to respond to events, and to those who approached him, for privileges, favour or sometimes justice, but he rarely initiated proceedings. Furthermore, between 1155 and 1178 he was an absentee for, in total, 14 years out of the 23, and when he was north of the Alps his primary concern was simply to keep the peace. Whereas in Italy he promulgated legislation, above all the Roncaglia decrees of 1158, the only German equivalent was the very infrequent attempts to impose a 'land peace', of which there were only three examples during the entire reign, one of which was soon after his accession and another right at the end, before his departure on crusade. Furthermore, the only other such peace, issued in February 1179, applied only to a very restricted, and carefully delineated, area of western Franconia. And while this was certainly an attempt to limit local violence and protect non-combatants, what it permitted was just as significant as what it forbade. It was to last for two years only. Men were allowed to fight in the open field but not to pursue their enemies into villages. Such warfare was only to take place from Mondays to Wednesdays. Peasants were not to carry arms outside their own villages, except for swords (which presumably few of them had). This 'peace' did not, therefore, seek to ban violence and feuding, but only to restrict its impact.[21] Unless we are to assume that there were many other such local edicts that no longer survive, which seems implausible, this was surely a response to a specific local problem, but we have no further information about the circumstances that led to its issue.

It is also indicative that while over a thousand documents written in Frederick's name survive, more than half of these are formal privileges, most of which are confirmations of existing

property and rights – mainly, as one might expect, to churches.
Almost all of these were granted in response to a request by the
recipient. This was despite the fact that the practical utility of
such documents seems to have been limited. Privileges granted
by a previous ruler were often ignored when a new one was
written, nor were privileges necessarily cited in legal disputes to
which they might have appeared relevant, and neither was attention always paid to them when they *were* produced in evidence.
What was really important was the conferment of such a privilege by the ruler as a sign of his favour and protection. It was
the ceremony of presenting the privilege that mattered, but for
this to be effective it needed to be done in the recipient's own
locality, to be witnessed by the important men of the region. The
grant of a privilege to a church in Swabia, for example, needed
to be done in Swabia, where it would have maximum public
effect. Conferment in another region would have virtually no
visibility and no impact. Hence the importance of the emperor
travelling around the country and going to the localities, where
local petitioners could approach him and receive his privileges.
It was important for the emperor that he should be seen in
person to manifest his authority, but it was also important for
those who received his privileges that their neighbours – and
especially their enemies – could see him granting these, so that
they could see his favour being manifested. By contrast, only
about a hundred of Frederick's known documents are mandates:
that is, documents instructing somebody to do something, perhaps to render justice in a dispute, or to reinstate somebody with
rights that had been lost or usurped by another, or to cease
attacking another party. An interesting, if not necessarily typ-
ical, example of this type of document came in summer 1178,
when Frederick instructed Margrave Otto of Brandenburg to
assist the Bishop of Verden in a boundary dispute. The relatively
peremptory tone of this mandate, addressed to one of the princes,

was unusual, but so were the circumstances. The Bishop of Halberstadt had initiated a case at the papal Curia concerning the boundaries of their respective dioceses. The margrave was told to assist the Bishop of Verden, a loyal subject of the empire, who had been 'vainly calumniated' by his fellow bishop.[22] What was not said here, but which underlay this case, was that Ulrich of Halberstadt had been a supporter of Alexander III during the schism. He had spent many years in exile as a result and had only been reinstated as part of the peace agreement of 1177. The appeal to the pope on an essentially secular issue was in itself an affront to the emperor's dignity, by someone whom he considered an enemy and whose reinstatement he was only reluctantly prepared to tolerate. This mandate was not therefore an instruction to render impartial justice, but to assist one of the emperor's friends. In this case, since the margrave and his family were allies of the emperor, and (as we shall see) needed his support at this time, the mandate probably had an effect. But in most cases we do not know whether such instructions were put into practice.

Where the emperor rendered justice at his court, the decision in such cases was intended to be consensual. Whichever members of the great and good of the realm were present would consult with the emperor to bring an end to the case, frequently by compromise, and with Frederick acting less as a judge than as the chairman, coordinating the decision, which, it would be emphasized, was by the consent of those present. Particularly where the persons involved were among the other great men of the kingdom, there would often be an attempt to save the 'honour' – that is, the public reputation – of both parties. Underlying such attempts was the knowledge that those seeking what they considered justice might well resort to violence, for the feud was still considered a means to justice in twelfth-century Germany. While this was to be avoided if possible, the means to do so was not to shame or disparage one party – unless he was blatantly in the wrong, or of such limited importance that his humiliation did not matter. Even then, there were usually limits. So when Frederick heard a complaint by the monks of a Cistercian monastery in the diocese of Toul, in upper Lotharingia, at Basle in September 1174, the defendant, a noble who had plundered the monastery and was clearly in the wrong, received a stiff dressing-down but was then forgiven provided that he did not offend again. 'After he had been reviled and bitterly denounced with many harsh and angry words before the princes of the court, we were quite merciful to him, thanks to our higher regard for collective peace and love.' That he could produce influential guarantors as to his future behaviour, the Archbishop of Trier and Werner of Bolanden, a wealthy imperial *ministerialis*, did him no harm.[23]

The procedure at such courts, and the operation of justice as a whole, was ad hoc and far from routine. There was no established system, as there was in contemporary England, for the king to issue a mandate ordering one of his own officials to do justice to a plaintiff in a local court, nor for parties in a local legal dispute to appeal to the royal court against the decision of a lower court, for there was no hierarchy of royal courts, as there was in England or Sicily – the two most 'advanced' governments of the day. In Germany, justice at the local level was privatized, and princes and local magnates would have taken an appeal to the Crown against their justice very badly – not that this occurred. Furthermore, one vestige of the old Ottonian-era provincial duchies that survived was that each province retained its own laws and procedure. A case heard under Swabian law, for example, could not be heard outside Swabia. And cases which were heard before the royal court were decided by the princes and nobles present, without the involvement of professional judges, as would have been the case in the contemporary kingdoms of

Sicily and England. There is no sign that Frederick sought to change any of this, or to develop any royal administration apart from that of the Crown's own lands or those of his family, which is what the other princes were also doing. Indeed, the emperor was happy to devolve governmental functions to the princes, as for example in his grant of the frontier bishoprics to Henry the Lion in 1154, the privilege creating the Duchy of Austria in 1156, or his concession of ducal authority, including the exercise of justice, throughout his extensive diocese to the Bishop of Würzburg in July 1168.[24] Similarly, he displayed a benign neglect towards the eastwards expansion of the Reich's frontiers by the princes of eastern Saxony, not just by Henry the Lion but by the Wettins and the landgraves of Thuringia, as well as by lesser dynasts like the counts of Holstein. The emperor's concern, and especially in the years up to 1177 when his attention was concentrated on Italy, was above all to retain the great men of Germany as his allies and supporters and to prevent any major rifts breaking out among them. 'Collective peace and love', at least among the people who mattered politically, was the primary function of Frederick's government. In the years after 1178, however, that ideal was to be severely tested.

FIVE

The Last Years, 1178–90

When Frederick returned to Germany in October 1178, trouble was already brewing in Saxony as a fresh coalition gathered against Henry the Lion. In the years since 1170, when the emperor's support had preserved the duke's position against his numerous local enemies, his position in Saxony had, if anything, become stronger, while his pretensions had certainly increased. Henry's reputation, not just within Germany but as a figure of international significance, had already been shown by his marriage in 1168 to Matilda, daughter of King Henry II of England. (She was then 12; Henry was at least 35, if not older.) On his way to the Holy Land in 1172 he had been received by Emperor Manuel Komnenos at Constantinople with elaborate ceremony, and – according to the later, but well-informed, account of Arnold of Lübeck – as though he was a visiting monarch, being seated beside the emperor while Mass was celebrated. He was similarly feted by the Turkish sultan of Asia Minor, Kilij-Arslan, on his return journey.[1] Henry's daughter by his first marriage was betrothed to the eldest son of King Waldemar of Denmark in 1171, and soon after the marriage had taken place, in 1177 the duke and Waldemar conducted a joint campaign into the Slav regions of Pomerania and Mecklenburg. Meanwhile the duke created his own palace complex at Brunswick, on a larger scale than the palace built by Barbarossa at Gelnhausen, and with a substantial collegiate church attached

Saxony in the reign of Frederick Barbarossa.

to it on which work began in 1175. Henry's self-image can be seen from the illuminated Gospel book created for him at the monastery of Helmarshausen during this decade, in which he was extolled as a descendant of Charlemagne and in a dedicatory picture he and his wife were portrayed with their illustrious

royal ancestors, Emperor Lothar, his grandfather and Henry II
and the latter's mother, Empress Matilda (wife of Henry V). This
consciousness of his quasi-royal status may have triggered the
hubris that led the duke into a series of fatal missteps, above all
the alienation of his cousin Frederick Barbarossa.

The first sign of the trouble that was to engulf Saxony was a
consequence of the peace agreement between the emperor and
Alexander III. The schismatic Bishop of Halberstadt, Gero, an
ally of the duke, was deposed and the former bishop, Ulrich, long
in exile because of his loyalty to Alexander, was restored. As soon
as he returned to Saxony, he demanded that the duke surrender
the fiefs that Gero had previously granted him. The duke refused,
Ulrich excommunicated him, and he retaliated by destroying
one of the episcopal castles. The bishop was supported by his
metropolitan, Archbishop Philip of Cologne, who had his own
reasons for opposing the duke. Philip had a personal grievance
against Henry, as a result of the latter's seizure of the inheritance
of Count Otto of Assel on the latter's death without children,
sometime after 1170. The count's widow was Philip's sister, and
he sought the inheritance, a substantial complex of estates east
of Hildesheim, for her – and perhaps ultimately for his see. More
generally, the archbishop had ambitions to extend the possessions
and power of Cologne into western Saxony. In the summer of
1178 he invaded Westphalia but was persuaded to withdraw by
Archbishop Wichmann of Magdeburg, who arranged a truce.
Soon afterwards the emperor returned to Germany, and both duke
and archbishop hastened to a diet at Speyer in early November
1178, there to launch mutual complaints as to the other's behaviour. But, ominously for Henry, other princes also made
accusations against him. The emperor postponed hearing these
until a further diet, to be held at Worms in two months' time.

Arnold of Lübeck suggested that Frederick was deliberately
dissimulating and was intending to harm the duke by summoning

Collegiate Church of Sts Blaise and John the Baptist, Brunswick.

him to Worms specifically to answer the charges against him, because he wanted to punish Henry for his refusal to assist him in Italy three years earlier: 'When Caesar saw that the princes intended to harm him, using great sagacity he turned all his efforts towards securing the duke's overthrow.'[2] That may have been true, or was it perhaps a subsequent rationalization in the light of Henry's eventual downfall? Frederick doubtless resented the duke's failure to support him, especially given the disastrous consequences of the Legnano campaign. If we can trust the various accounts of their meeting at Chiavenna in 1176, the emperor had not just requested but begged Henry on his knees for his assistance, and while such supplication was highly ritualized, it was unheard of for a ruler who resorted to such an extreme measure to be refused. Why, then, had Henry rejected this plea? We can hardly take Arnold of Lübeck seriously when he claimed that the duke had pleaded advanced age for his reluctance to take part – he was, after all, between seven and ten years younger than the emperor. More plausibly, Otto of

Henry the Lion alongside his wife Matilda of England and their
ancestors, illumination from the Gospels of Henry the Lion, *c.* 1188.

St Blasien suggested that in return for his military assistance
Henry had demanded that the emperor grant him Goslar as a
fief, but that Frederick had refused to be blackmailed.[3] If so, then
Henry's greed had outdistanced his prudence.

Duke Henry failed to attend the Worms diet of January
1179. This may have been because he feared the charges against
him – it may also have been pique because it was at that meeting
that the final agreement between the emperor and Welf vi was
concluded that secured the latter's inheritance for Frederick
and his sons. Henry also failed to attend a further meeting, held
at Magdeburg in June, when Margrave Dietrich of Landsberg,
one of the duke's old enemies, accused him of treason and challenged him, in his absence, to a judicial duel. In response to
the princes' demands Henry was then outlawed.[4] At this point
the duke seems to have backtracked and sought a private meeting with the emperor. But Frederick would only agree to mediate
between him and his princely enemies in return for an enormous

gift of 5,000 marks, which the duke was too proud, or too stingy, to pay – or perhaps he doubted whether such expenditure would achieve anything. He may also have reckoned that he had had sufficient military resources to fight off any attack – which at first seemed to be the case. For while the sentence of outlawry allowed his numerous enemies to attack him with impunity, to overthrow him was no easy task. An army led by Philip of Cologne invaded southeastern Saxony but became bogged down in besieging the duke's fortress at Haldensleben and broke up in disarray, with the allies bickering among themselves. Henry retaliated by capturing Halberstadt and Bishop Ulrich, and during the sack which followed much of the town was burned down. Meanwhile Henry also sent his troops into Westphalia, where they inflicted a sharp defeat on the archbishop's allies near Osnabrück, in which Count Simon of Tecklenburg and a number of other leading men were captured. Militarily, therefore, the campaign of autumn 1179 had done nothing to damage the duke's position.

In retrospect, however, these months still sealed the duke's fate. First, at a further diet at Würzburg in January 1180, the princes declared that as a contumacious vassal who had three times refused the emperor's summons Henry had forfeited his ducal titles, his fiefs and (perhaps) his allodial land as well. At a further meeting at Gelnhausen in April Frederick then regranted Saxony, splitting it into two duchies. Westphalia was given to Archbishop Philip and the church of Cologne, eastern Saxony to Bernhard of Anhalt, one of the sons of Albrecht the Bear, who had (as we have seen) a hereditary claim to the ducal title, and who (unlike Henry) had joined the emperor in Italy in 1176.[5] Finally, in September 1180, at an assembly at Altenburg in the Pleissenland, Bavaria was given to Frederick's old and trusted friend Otto of Wittelsbach, although what Otto received was somewhat less than Henry had held as duke. Styria was raised from a frontier march into a separate duchy, and a further duchy, Merania, was created for the eldest son of Count Berthold of Andechs, from the other main noble family in Bavaria apart from the Wittelsbach. Berthold the elder was another loyal and long-serving supporter of the emperor, who had taken part in three of the five Italian expeditions and been made margrave of Istria in 1173. This new duchy was located in Dalmatia (on the Adriatic coast of modern Croatia), but the Andechs family also possessed a strong landed base in Bavaria. Once Henry the Lion's titles and lands had been granted to others, it would have been very difficult to return to the situation before the crisis, which was no doubt why his enemies insisted that Frederick proceed with these confiscations. Second, although victorious in the autumn of 1179, Duke Henry squandered his advantage by falling out with his leading followers, especially concerning who was to have custody of the various prisoners taken (and of their ransoms). During 1180 two of his principal allies, counts Adolf of Holstein and Bernhard of Ratzeburg, both formidable soldiers, defected to his enemies.

Nevertheless, the duke continued to put up fierce resistance. A first campaign in the summer of 1180 miscarried, and Frederick's nephews, Ludwig of Thuringia and his brother Hermann, newly installed as Count Palatine of Saxony, were captured. It was clear that Frederick himself needed to become involved and not merely leave the fighting to others. Although it is probable that many of his troops were provided by Henry's east Saxon enemies, Frederick was able to turn the tide in a six-week campaign from late July to early September, during which he captured several of the duke's most important castles. Even more important, many of the Saxon nobles who had hitherto remained loyal to the duke, and some of his *ministeriales*, were reluctant to fight directly against the emperor and also anxious not to lose their lands, and submitted during the autumn. Furthermore, the Slav lords of Pomerania, hitherto Henry's

allies, also changed sides. It still took a further campaign the
next year finally to secure victory. Haldensleben, the key fortress
left to the duke in southern Saxony, surrendered to Archbishop
Wichmann in May 1181, while in July and August the emperor
himself mopped up most of what was left in Henry's hands in
the region north of the Elbe, assisted by the king of Denmark
and his fleet. Henry himself surrendered in November. He was
allowed to retain his allodial land around Brunswick and
Lüneburg – here the original sentence against him may have
been softened – but had to agree to go into exile, which he did
in July 1182. He and most of his family spent three years with his
father-in-law King Henry in England and Normandy, before he
eventually returned to Germany in August 1185.

The downfall of Henry the Lion has often been accounted a
victory for the emperor, but in some respects it was a very cir-
cumscribed one. Admittedly, it removed by far the most powerful
of the German princes, whose position in north Germany enabled him to behave increasingly independently of the emperor's
authority. (Bavaria was always less of a problem, since Henry's
own holdings within the duchy were not extensive, and he spent
relatively little time there.) But Frederick did not profit directly
from his fall. The fiefs confiscated from Henry were redistributed
to those who had brought him down. It was once thought that
there was a legal requirement for fiefs held from the emperor to
be regranted within a year (the so-called *Leihezwang*), which
forced Frederick to do this, but this seems improbable – it was
rather the pragmatic need to reward the princes and other enemies of the duke – and later jurists from the thirteenth century
onwards took this as a precedent and developed the concept of
compulsory re-enfeoffment. But in another sense the princes
were able to force Frederick's hand. While it looks as though he
wanted to reduce the power of his over-mighty subject, he may
not have sought Henry's disinheritance on the scale that took

place. In a letter to the duke some years later, after the latter's return to Germany, Frederick claimed that his downfall was not what he had sought but was the result of 'necessity', and that Henry's offences had made him 'intolerable' to the princes.[6] Was the offer to mediate between the duke and his enemies in 1179, albeit in return for payment, therefore merely a sham, or was it a serious offer? That may not have mattered – Henry had too many enemies who hated and feared him, or who, like Philip of Cologne, were anxious to benefit from his downfall. Arnold of Lübeck indeed claimed that Frederick had sworn an oath to the princes not to restore the duke to his former position without their consent, 'since all the princes were determined on his overthrow'.[7] That Henry was allowed to retain his ancestral lands round Brunswick was probably due to the emperor's own initiative, but that was the most that he could do for him. The term of his exile is also problematic – it may originally have been indefinite, but because in the end Henry returned after three years later chroniclers assumed that this must have been the sentence passed. But it is possible that he only returned because some of his erstwhile enemies changed their minds, above all Archbishop Philip – for reasons that will be discussed below.

The long-term consequence of Henry's downfall was a change in the nature of princely authority. With the split of the duchies of Saxony and Bavaria, the fragmentation of the old provincial duchies, which began as early as the late tenth century, was finally completed. The creation of new duchies increased the number of imperial princes, directly dependent upon the emperor, as did Frederick's enfeoffment of the Slav rulers of Pomerania and Mecklenburg, already Christian and partly Germanized, but who over the next couple of generations became completely acculturized, and their lands very much part of the Reich – although the Duchy of Mecklenburg was not formally created until 1348. And it was from the last years of Barbarossa's reign that a clear understanding developed of what princely status was – the emergence of the so-called *Reichsfürstenstand* (the guild of imperial princes) that became enshrined in the *Sachsenspiegel*, the key text of thirteenth-century German law. These princes were directly dependent on the emperor and on no other layman – they could only hold fiefs from the emperor or churchmen, a status known in German as *Reichsunmittelbarkeit*. It also became customary that new princes could only be admitted to this rank through the formal recognition of their status by the emperor, with the consent of the other princes. It is possible, although not absolutely certain, that the first time this occurred was with the creation of the Margraviate of Namur by Frederick in 1184.

One might see the fragmentation of the old duchies and the increase in the number of princes as something that worked to the advantage of the emperor, although several princely families (Ascanians, Wettins, Wittelsbach) held more than one position, and Frederick later consented to the Duke of Austria inheriting Styria when its childless duke died, which he did in 1192. (At Frederick's death there were 22 lay princes, but from only 15 families.) But the extent of Frederick's authority in Germany after 1180 is problematic. Was he responsible for the fall of Henry the Lion, or was he a pawn of the other princes? Frederick's itinerary and court may also suggest that his authority was diminishing. From 1168 onwards Frederick only rarely ventured north of the river Main, with the exception of his campaigns in Saxony during 1179–81, and visits to the Pleissenland. His itinerary was otherwise almost entirely limited to Franconia, Swabia and Alsace. Nor after 1178 did he visit Burgundy, although the empress spent some considerable time in that region before her death in 1184 and King Henry made a brief visit there in 1188. Regensburg continued to be a regular destination during the 1180s, but otherwise Frederick did not enter Bavaria. For an example of this restricted itinerary we may look at one of the last years of his reign.

He spent Christmas 1186 at Nuremberg, then cannot be traced until mid-March, when he was at Regensburg, where he celebrated Easter (29 March). From there he went to Augsburg in early April, then to Donauwörth, travelling about 400 kilometres (250 mi.) westwards across northern Swabia to Alsace, spending Whitsun (17 May) in Toul. He seems to have remained in Alsace for about two months, before spending two weeks in August at Worms, and then at nearby Kaiserslautern, before going south to Konstanz, where he can be attested at the end of September. He then returned to Alsace, reaching Straßburg, 177 kilometres (110 mi.) from Konstanz, by 1 December, where he held a diet and met the papal legate, Cardinal Henry of Albano, to discuss the prospects for a crusade; then meeting King Philip of France on the river Meuse near Mouzon, about 240 kilometres (150 mi.) west, probably for the same reason, and finally spending Christmas at Trier, his first visit there for many years, but necessary because of a long-running dispute about the archbishopric. The distances travelled were certainly less than in the earlier years of the reign, though still impressive for a man in his mid-sixties. But, apart from the meeting with King Philip, he had not ventured out of the Staufen heartland.

If the itinerary had changed, so had those who attended the emperor. By the 1180s the lay princes rarely attended Frederick's court, apart from those who were closely related to him: his sons, his brother Conrad and his nephew Ludwig of Thuringia. Even his other nephew, Duke Simon of Upper Lotharingia, can only be attested once at court during this decade. The dukes of Carinthia, for example, never came to court. Nor were the bishops as assiduous in attending upon the emperor as they had been earlier. Even the Swabian bishops rarely attended, although this may be explicable as a reaction to the emperor's territorial aggrandizement within the duchy, which potentially threatened the material interests of their sees. One of the few exceptions, who was regularly at court, was Otto of Andechs, Bishop of Bamberg from 1177 to 1196, who was from a family that had benefited greatly from their close association with the emperor. A few of the lesser aristocracy frequently attended the emperor, such as Counts Henry of Dietz (in Hesse), Count Albrecht of Hildenberg, Conrad Burgrave of Nuremberg and the sons of

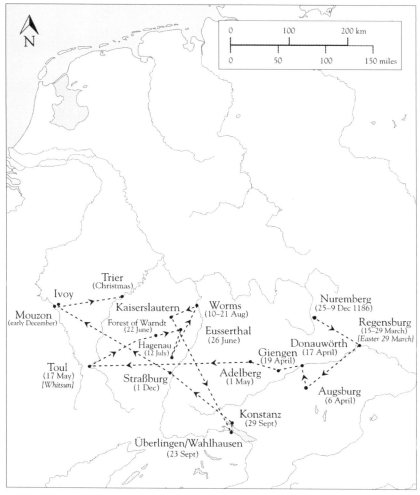

Frederick I's itinerary in Germany, 1187.

another Franconian noble, Markward of Grumbach, who had himself been a loyal servant of the emperor until his death in 1172 – all of whom were to go on Frederick's crusade – but even these were relatively few. Increasingly prominent, however, were a number of imperial *ministeriales*, such as the marshal Henry of Kalden and Werner of Bolanden, both also from Franconia. Another such *ministerialis*, Markward of Annweiler, from Alsace, was equally prominent at the court of the young King Henry – he was to become the latter's right-hand man after 1190. Werner was probably the richest *ministerialis* in Germany, possessing, according to Gilbert of Mons, seventeen castles and many vassals of his own.[8] Nevertheless, he was important because of his proximity to the emperor, not in his own right. That men of his rank now played such a significant role in the emperor's entourage was because their social superiors did not. This trend was to become even more marked during the reign of Henry VI.

The one occasion when the great and good of the Reich were assembled was at the royal court held outside Mainz at Pentecost in May 1184, where Frederick had his two eldest sons knighted, and then walked in solemn procession with his wife and eldest son, all three wearing crowns, as a very clear and public sign that Henry was his designated successor. This was attended by most of the prelates and 'a joyful crowd of princes and a host of nobles, all jealously anxious to please the emperor'.[9] Gilbert of Mons named twelve lay princes, six archbishops, seventeen bishops and three prominent abbots who attended this diet, and (implausibly) estimated that their followings were so numerous that 70,000 knights were also present.[10] This was certainly a spectacular demonstration of Frederick's personal authority and prestige, but it was also decidedly unusual. And even here there were a couple of conspicuous absentees, namely the Archbishop of Salzburg and the Duke of Carinthia. So although the emperor's cousin Leopold of Austria *was* present, representation from the southeast of the Reich, the area which had been least loyal during the schism, was limited.

When Henry the Lion departed into exile in 1182 Frederick was almost sixty, having already lived to a greater age than almost all his predecessors on the imperial throne. Three issues were to dominate his last years: ensuring his son's succession, stabilizing and if possible salvaging the imperial position in Italy, and dealing with various problems with the Church, both within Germany and, more crucially, with the papacy – these were, however, two aspects of the same problem. Finally, in the autumn of 1187 the news of the capture of the Holy Land by Saladin superseded other issues, as the need for a new Crusading expedition became central to the politics of Christendom.

Though Henry had been designated king as a small child, the knighthood and crown-wearing at Mainz marked his transition to adulthood and was the first step to consolidating his position as the generally acknowledged next ruler. Soon afterwards Henry was left as the temporary ruler of Germany when Frederick returned to Italy for the sixth and final time in September 1184. But a year earlier, while still north of the Alps, Frederick had taken his most crucial step in regularizing his relations with the Italian communes. The peace of Venice had specified only a six-year truce between the emperor and the Lombard League, but as the expiry date of that truce approached, both sides sought a permanent peace. The details were worked out in a series of preliminary talks with Frederick's envoys, principally at Piacenza in April 1183. These were then embodied in a treaty concluded at Konstanz on 25 June 1183. Although drafted as an imperial privilege, granted by the emperor out of his goodness, it largely embodied the terms that the Lombard cities desired to secure their self-government. The cities were to exercise the regalian rights that Frederick had once been keen to exploit. Those that legitimately pertained to the emperor would be identified by

Barbarossa and his two eldest sons, illumination from the Weingartner
Welfenchronik, *c.* 1185.

sworn inquests – alternatively the league could pay him 2,000
marks a year to exercise those rights that would otherwise be
his. All privileges granted during the previous conflict that
harmed the cities' rights were to be null and void, and judicial
sentences against former rebels would be disregarded. Appeals to

the emperor in legal cases concerning property would be allowed, but such cases must be heard by his representatives in Italy, and nobody should be forced to travel to Germany to secure justice. Above all, the Lombard League was formally recognized, and previous agreements between individual members should remain in force. Finally, the emperor specifically recognized the rights of Milan to possess Seprio and two other counties that had previously been in dispute and confiscated from it, although the Milanese also agreed not to intrude on the territory of Lodi. This was, therefore, a comprehensive settlement of the issues that had been in dispute, and it was laid down that not only would a nominee of the emperor swear in his name faithfully to observe the terms of the agreement, but so too would his sons and ten named prelates, seven dukes and three other imperial princes.[11] (The emperor's nominee who swore the oath was, significantly, an imperial *ministerialis*, and among the named witnesses to the treaty were several others, including Werner of Bolanden.)

Yet while the treaty of Konstanz effectively guaranteed the freedom of the Lombard cities, one should note that it was not a complete surrender by the emperor and that certain imperial rights were also guaranteed. While Frederick agreed not to make overlong stays in individual cities, his right to visit them was maintained, and the *fodrum* could still be levied to support his following. Although the cities had the right to elect their own consuls, these should be men who had previously sworn fealty to the emperor and should be invested by him or his local representatives in his name, and such investitures should be renewed every five years. And, as we have seen, the emperor would receive financial compensation for the loss of his legitimate regalian rights – though these would presumably have been those in force before 1158 rather than the wider powers claimed after the diet of Roncaglia. It was probably the best deal that could be obtained under the circumstances. One should note, however, that this agreement only affected relations with the Lombard cities. The empire was still very much in control in Tuscany, Romagna and the Marche, thanks in particular to the effective administration of Archbishop Christian of Mainz until his death in 1183.

When Frederick went to Italy a year later it became even clearer how much his previous policy had changed. He took only a small force with him – this was a diplomatic, not a military, campaign. The first city that he visited was Milan, once his great arch-enemy, and he then visited Verona, one of the progenitors of the league, and spent Christmas at Brescia, another city that had been consistently hostile to him. And in February 1185 he granted a privilege to Milan in which he conceded that city all his regalian rights both in its historic territory and in five other named counties, in return for an annual payment of 300 pounds of silver, and he even agreed not to make alliances with other cities without the consent of the Milanese. The latter also swore to observe the terms, not just to Frederick but to his son King Henry.[12] So Frederick had now completely reversed course in Lombardy, relying on friendship with Milan as the cornerstone of his policy. This was made even more obvious when Henry was summoned to Italy and in January 1186 was married to Constance of Sicily and crowned king of Italy in the monastery of St Ambrogio in Milan. Here Frederick both honoured his new allies and took a further step in entrenching the royal succession.

The marriage with Constance, recognized as the heiress to the Kingdom of Sicily, marked a further reversal of Frederick's policy, although the groundwork had been laid at Venice in 1177 when a long truce had been concluded between these two previously implacably hostile powers. Constance was the aunt of King William II of Sicily, although she was in fact a year younger than her nephew, being the last and posthumously born child of King Roger. The marriage was to have momentous consequences, although it is unlikely that these were foreseen at the time. While Constance was proclaimed the heiress to the kingdom, King William was still a young man, and his wife only twenty, so they could be expected to have children who would then inherit. What the king of Sicily stood to gain from this alliance is clear: both enhanced legitimacy for his kingdom as part of the top table of Christian monarchy and security from potential attack, which was important given William II's ambitious policy of Mediterranean expansion – which included an attack on Byzantium in 1185. Had Henry not already been betrothed to Constance by then, would the Sicilian monarchy have dared to undertake such a significant external military commitment? How the empire gained is less clear, given that the prospect of Constance and her husband actually succeeding to the kingdom must have appeared quite slim. The union also had the defect that the bride was 31, eleven years older than her husband, and this must have raised questions about her suitability for child bearing, which was, after all, the primary function of a medieval queen. It may be that Barbarossa felt that an alliance with Sicily, which had been the papacy's main political ally during the schism, would help to bring pressure to bear on the pope, at a time when relations with the empire were once more deteriorating.

To begin with, at least, the peace of Venice seemed as though it might introduce genuine amity and cooperation between emperor and pope. Soon afterwards the troops of Christian of Mainz helped to reinstall Alexander III in Rome and secure the surrender of the antipope Calixtus. Alexander was then able to hold a major Church council in Rome in March 1179, although a few months later his relations with the Romans became so difficult that he abandoned the city – and for most of the next decade the popes remained first in the Papal patrimony and then in northern Italy, without visiting Rome. Frederick's relations

with the next pope, Lucius III, a veteran cardinal who had been
close to Alexander, were also initially quite cordial, and the
emperor enthusiastically endorsed the pope's intention to attack
heresy. But by late 1184 all was not well between them. The problem was that the agreement at Venice may have ended the schism
but it had not solved all the issues left in its wake. The most
intractable was the status of the Matildine lands in the Romagna
and central Italy, but there was also a more general problem of
imperial financial levies, both on the clergy in northern Italy and
in the territory which the papacy claimed in central Italy, such
as Umbria and the Marche, in which the emperor considered
that he was still entitled to levy the *fodrum* and exercise his regalian rights. Nor, except in a few high-profile cases, had the 1177
agreement solved the problem of the validity of clerical appoint-
ments made by schismatics. On this last issue, Lucius III was at
first accommodating but then proceeded to make difficulties. The
pope also flatly refused Frederick's request that he should crown
his son as co-emperor. Furthermore, the emergence of problems
with the Church in Germany also complicated relations with
the papacy, in particular a disputed election to the archbishopric
of Trier in 1183 and a quarrel between Frederick and his former
chancellor, Archbishop Philip of Cologne, that developed a year
later. The Trier election dispute, initially an internal one within
the cathedral chapter, became so bitter and prolonged (it lasted
six years) because one of the candidates, Rudolf, appealed to
Frederick, who invested him with the regalia (the temporal rights
of the see), while the other, Folmar, appealed to the pope, who
not surprisingly favoured his candidacy. Matters were made worse
by a clumsy intervention by King Henry in December 1184,
while his father was in Italy, attempting to intimidate the chapter
to accept the imperial candidate by destroying the property of
those who opposed him. Underlying the dispute was the emperor's claim, in accordance with the concordat agreed at Worms

in 1122, to have the right to decide disputed elections, while the pope considered that this was a strictly ecclesiastical matter that ought to pertain to him.

The quarrel with Philip of Cologne had begun with an apparently minor issue, an unseemly dispute about precedence between the archbishop and the abbot of Fulda at the Mainz diet in May 1184. The furious archbishop had threatened to abandon the council and had to be calmed down, in public, by both Frederick and King Henry – the latter for once displaying some tact, although his actions during the Trier dispute and on several later occasions suggest that this was not his most characteristic quality.[13] Medieval aristocrats – Philip's father was a count – were notoriously touchy about their honour and prestige, and sensitive to perceived slights, but underlying this dispute may have been the archbishop's opposition to the emperor's acceptance of the new Margrave of Namur as an imperial prince. He appears to have seen this as a threat to the territorial pre-eminence of the see of Cologne in lower Lotharingia. He may therefore have been in a mood to cause trouble, at what Frederick intended as a showcase event for his rule. This may also explain his, at first sight surprising, support for the recall of Henry the Lion. Arnold of Lübeck, however, said that the real cause of the breach was a somewhat later row between King Henry and Philip, after the archbishop had arrested some merchants from Duisburg (a trading rival to Cologne) and confiscated their goods. He had ignored several orders from the king to restore this property and then made disparaging remarks about Henry. While Philip was eventually forced to give way and to pay 300 marks to recover the king's grace, he resented this and was thus estranged from both the emperor and his son.[14] Certainly by 1186 Archbishop Philip was openly opposing the emperor and his son, and positioning himself as a spokesman for the liberties of the clergy – he was especially critical of the traditional right

of 'spoil', by which the ruler enjoyed the income of a vacant
bishopric and the movable property of a deceased prelate.

Relations with the Church deteriorated further with the
death of Lucius III in November 1185 and the election of Uberto
Crivelli, Archbishop of Milan, as Urban III. If Lucius had been
increasingly unhappy and obstructive, Urban was actively hostile
to the emperor. He took an increasingly hard line, both with
regard to the rival territorial and jurisdictional claims in Italy
and in the Trier dispute and with regard to the controversy about
the right of spoil. And in summer 1186 he appointed Philip of
Cologne papal legate in Germany, which in the circumstances
must be seen as a deliberate act of provocation. He also consecrated his candidate, Folmar, as Archbishop of Trier. Frederick
retaliated by closing the Alpine passes to prevent papal envoys
coming to Germany. Admittedly, most of the German bishops
still remained loyal to Frederick. Archbishop Conrad of Mainz
and seven other German bishops were with him in Italy in 1185–6,
although not all necessarily at the same time, on what was a relatively small-scale expedition. And after a council at Gelnhausen
in November 1186 the archbishops of Magdeburg and Salzburg
wrote to the pope defending Frederick's conduct, albeit in very
respectful terms, and seeking a negotiated settlement which would
take account of the emperor's reasonable claims.[15] The sources
vary as to what the upshot of all this was – some suggest that there
were constructive negotiations during 1187, while by contrast
the Marbach annalist, from the Staufen heartland in Alsace,
claimed that Urban was preparing to excommunicate the
emperor, but that 'God prevented his evil plan.'[16]

This allegedly divine intervention took two forms. First
there was the appalling news that Saladin had comprehensively
defeated the army of the Kingdom of Jerusalem and his forces
were busy capturing the cities and castles of the Holy Land.
Second, Pope Urban died at Ferrara on 20 October. (Whether

the one event caused the other, as some contemporaries alleged, cannot, of course, be proven.) Soon afterwards news arrived that the city of Jerusalem had fallen into Muslim hands – it surrendered to Saladin on 2 October 1187. The loss of the Holy Land led to an immediate call for a new crusade to recover for Christianity the land where Christ had once trodden. The new pope, Gregory VIII, issued a summons to this effect in his bull *Audita Tremendi* (On Hearing of the Dreadful News) on 29 October only a week after his election – with a speed which suggests that drafting the call may have already begun in the last weeks of his predecessor's pontificate. In these circumstances the need for peace within Christendom was paramount, and previous disputes had become irrelevant. If the Holy Land was to be recovered, the emperor's participation was clearly not just desirable but necessary. The immediate despatch of a senior cardinal as legate to Germany, his meeting with the emperor at Straßburg and the conference with the king of France, all before the end of the year, showed the urgency of the situation, and how much papal relations with the emperor had been changed by the news from the Holy Land.

It is possible that Frederick had already been contemplating once again taking the cross. During a meeting with Pope Lucius at Verona in November 1184 he had met a high-level delegation from the East, headed by Heraclius, Patriarch of Jerusalem, which had embarked on a tour of Western Europe seeking aid against the growing threat posed by Saladin, and had apparently been sympathetic to their pleas. How serious he may have been at this point is, however, questionable. He was still embroiled in problems with the Church – which the Verona meeting did nothing to solve – and other rulers also made sympathetic responses to the envoys from Jerusalem without necessarily intending to do much about this, notably Henry II of England. Furthermore, this was only one among a series of appeals for help from the Frankish states in the east, stretching back for a number of years, and all pleading the desperate state of affairs there. While the threat from an increasingly unified Islamic world to the Christian states in the east *was* growing, the lack of response from the west may have been the result of a perception that the Franks of the east were crying wolf too often. The fall of Jerusalem and most of its kingdom brutally brought home the seriousness of the situation to the Christian west.

Frederick himself took the cross at a council held in Mainz in March 1188, on *Laetare* Sunday, the third Sunday before Easter, which was the anniversary of his coronation 36 years earlier. (The anthem for that Sunday, 'Rejoice (*laetare*) Jerusalem', was especially associated with the crusade.) His expedition left from Regensburg in May 1189. The considerable delay before his army departed for the Holy Land was not, however, wasted or the result of needless procrastination. As a young man, Frederick had taken part in the crusade of Conrad III which had suffered from poor planning and inadequate preparation, and he was determined not to repeat his uncle's mistakes. The intervening period was devoted not only to an intensive recruiting campaign and preparation within Germany, and to the settlement of problems there, but also to diplomatic initiatives to ensure as smooth a passage to the east as possible. The initial recruitment had begun at Straßburg in December 1187, where we are told that the preaching 'roused the minds of many men of distinction to undertake the journey of Christ. These men enthusiastically took the sign of the Cross there, and they gloriously set an example for many others who piously imitated them thereafter.'[7] Among those who enlisted then was Bishop Gottfried of Würzburg, who before his election to that see had been Frederick's chancellor. But the greatest stimulus to recruitment was undoubtedly the assembly at Mainz, 'attended by all the great men of the German kingdom, both clergy and lay', where Frederick himself took the cross from

the Bishop of Würzburg and which was christened 'the court of
Jesus Christ'.[18] And at this same assembly various disputes that
might potentially destabilize the kingdom were settled, most
crucially that between the emperor himself and the Archbishop
of Cologne, as well as another long-running feud between the
Bishop of Utrecht and the Count of Geldern. Not only would
such disputes potentially hinder recruiting, but they would make
it much more difficult for the emperor to depart for what might
well be several years. An equally important purpose of the Mainz
council was once again publicly to display King Henry acting
alongside the emperor as the acknowledged future ruler. The
process of at least outward reconciliation was not, however,
necessarily easy. Philip of Cologne had been summoned to the
Straßburg meeting and had failed to attend – it may be because of
this that Frederick had not taken the cross at this earliest opportunity – and in the intervening months King Henry had tried,
albeit unsuccessfully, to recruit the nobles of lower Lotharingia
for a military campaign against the archbishop. But eventually
Philip agreed to pay 2,000 marks to recover the emperor's grace
and 260 more to the court, and offered to have the defences of
Cologne partly demolished, although the emperor graciously
remitted this last concession. The emperor also attempted to
solve another Low Countries dispute between Baldwin (v) of
Hainault and his uncle the Count of Namur, though here the
most he could do was to paper over the cracks of a quarrel that
also involved, among others, the Duke of Zähringen and the
Archbishop of Cologne, and was to continue to cause problems
for Henry vi after his own death. The most pressing problem
was, however, that posed by Henry the Lion, who despite the loss
of his fiefs and ducal title retained the potential to disrupt north
Germany. Frederick arranged a meeting at Goslar in late July
1188 where Henry was formally reconciled with his successor
as Duke of Saxony, Bernhard of Anhalt. Nevertheless, this was

not felt to be enough. Frederick therefore gave Henry three choices. He could be restored to a few of his lost lands and rights if he abandoned any claim to the rest. Alternatively, he could join the forthcoming crusade, at the end of which he would receive a larger part of his lost property. Or, finally, he and his eldest son could go into exile for another three years. Henry chose this last option – presumably reserving the right to attempt to reclaim his lost inheritance after that time.[19] Finally, to consolidate this process of peace-making, Frederick promulgated a land peace at his diet at Nuremberg on 29 December 1188 – although, like earlier such decrees, this was not a prohibition of warfare, but rather a set of rules to limit its impact, especially on non-combatants, and in particular to prevent arson during feuding.[20]

Furthermore, the papacy sought to solve, or at least downplay, the disputes which had so soured relations with the emperor since the early part of the decade. First Gregory VIII, during his brief two-month pontificate, and then Clement III, who succeeded him in December 1187, tried to damp down the Trier election dispute. Gregory forbade Folmar from excommunicating any of his opponents, reminding him that the Church needed the emperor and that he should do nothing to inflame the conflict further. Clement then sent legates to Germany in summer 1188 to enquire into the affair. Eventually he decided that for the sake of peace it would be better to annul the elections of both candidates, and finally, in autumn 1189, after Frederick's departure on crusade but at the request of King Henry, he confirmed the election of the imperial chancellor John as the new archbishop.[21] Meanwhile the emperor allowed Bishop Bertram of Metz, who had been expelled from his see for supporting Folmar, to return. Pope Clement was also prepared, from the beginning of his pontificate, to address King Henry as 'Roman emperor elect', although he did not receive his imperial coronation until

Barbarossa the Crusader, illumination from *Historia Hierosolymitana*,
c. 1188.

after his father's death. Other problems, above all that of the
Matildine lands, were not so easy to resolve, but at this stage
nobody wanted to make an issue of them.

A decision was taken early on that the expedition would take
the traditional land route to the Holy Land, through the Balkans
and Asia Minor to Palestine, following the example of the First
Crusade of 1096–9 and that of Conrad III of 1147–9. Bishop

Gottfried of Würzburg had argued that they should travel by sea, but neither the emperor nor Clement III were keen on this. Given the probable size of the expedition it was unlikely that there would have been sufficient shipping available, certainly at one go, and it was clearly undesirable that the army should arrive as a series of detachments over perhaps several months. Furthermore, with only a handful of ports along the Syrian coast still in Christian hands – and only Tyre in the Kingdom of Jerusalem – and all of these under threat, there was a justified fear that a maritime expedition might find itself with nowhere to land. It was also possible that an army marching by land could recruit along the way – as Frederick did indeed in Hungary. But to avoid the potential pitfalls of the long and arduous land journey, the emperor did everything he could in advance to ensure that his army would have an easy and unopposed passage for as long as it possibly could. As soon as he had taken the cross, Frederick sent Archbishop Conrad of Mainz to the king of Hungary, another embassy to Byzantium, and an imperial *ministerialis*, Gottfried of Wiesenbach, to the Seljuk sultan Kilij-Arslan, all of whom were tasked with securing unopposed passage and the provision of markets where the army could buy food. Another ambassador, Count Henry of Dietz, was sent to Saladin, to tell him to evacuate the Holy Land and to return the True Cross (a relic of the Crucifixion captured at the Battle of Hattin) to the Christians. Frederick can have had little hope that this last mission would have a favourable response, but since earlier in his reign he had been in communication with Saladin he sought to observe diplomatic niceties, by making a formal declaration of war. Hungary was a Christian kingdom, with which Frederick's relations in recent years had been good. Nor was it impossible that Kilij-Arslan would allow the expedition passage through his lands in Asia Minor. Although he was a Muslim, he was a rival rather than an ally of Saladin. Furthermore, in 1172 he had not only allowed Henry the Lion to travel unmolested through his lands on his return from his pilgrimage to Jerusalem but had entertained him as an honoured guest at his court. The sultan had also sent an embassy to the imperial court in 1179, and in response to Gottfried's mission he despatched envoys to Frederick who met the emperor at Nuremberg soon after Christmas 1188. A further Turkish envoy met the emperor during the crusade, while he was at Adrianople in Byzantine territory in February 1190, promising free passage and markets. But from the first the tricky negotiations were those with the Eastern Empire.

Emperor Isaac Angelos did at least respond to Frederick's embassy. His own counter-embassy, headed by John Doukas, Logothete of the Drome (the Byzantine foreign minister), reached Frederick at Nuremberg late in 1188. But there they found not only the Turkish envoys but also those of the Serb *zupan* Stephen Nemanja, who was then in revolt against Byzantium. Their report can have done nothing to reassure the Byzantine emperor. The Byzantines had never been comfortable with large, and often ill-disciplined, western armies marching through their territory and coming near their capital, Constantinople. The passage of Conrad III's army in 1147 had not gone well, with frequent plundering and several open clashes, even though he and Manuel Komnenos had been allies whose personal relations were remarkably friendly. Furthermore, there was always the suspicion that the westerners might use their concern for the Holy Land as cover for an attack on Constantinople. With the Eastern Empire now weaker than it had been under Manuel and much of the Balkans in rebellion, and having only recently repelled a major attack by the Kingdom of Sicily in 1185, the Byzantines had every reason to fear the arrival of the German emperor. His seemingly friendly relations with the recalcitrant Serbian prince can only have made matters worse. There was also the perennial problem of the 'two empires', each claiming to be the legitimate successor to the

Roman Empire of old and reluctant to recognize the imperial pretensions of the other. That Isaac also enjoyed friendly relations with Saladin, whom he saw as an ally against the Turks of Asia Minor, only made matters worse, although western reports that the two had concluded an alliance against the crusaders were probably mistaken.

Nevertheless, the talks at Nuremberg went well enough for Frederick to send a second, higher-profile, embassy to Constantinople in the spring of 1189, not long before the expedition set off, comprising Bishop Hermann of Münster, Count Rupert of Nassau – both of whom had served him long and faithfully – and his chamberlain, Markward of Neuenburg, another *ministerialis* from Franconia. They were to make sure that 'those things that had been promised on oath by the Greeks might actually be fulfilled by them and made ready for the army'. But, as the main contemporary historian of the expedition lamented, in the event they were 'sheep in the midst of wolves'.[22]

The year between the emperor taking the cross and his departure was also spent raising money – of which a great deal would be needed, not least to pay for food if markets were provided along the way in friendly territory. This was certainly preferable to simply commandeering supplies, which was a sure way to alienate the local population. Quite how such money was raised is by no means clear, although it is probable that both towns and churches contributed substantial sums to the emperor, as well as those like Philip of Cologne who paid to be restored to favour or to have privileges issued to them. But in contrast to the kingdoms of France and England, there was no general tax – the so-called 'Saladin tithe' – levied. Most participants were expected to finance themselves, at least in the first instance. Frederick instructed those taking part to prepare for an expedition lasting up to two years and expected even the poorest participants to have a minimum of three marks each to cover their expenses.

That certainly would not have been sufficient for such a long period – knights on expeditions to Italy during the reign needed a mark a month for their expenses, though they would probably have had to provide for servants too. Presumably the emperor would subsidize some of those involved after the early months. Given the size of the expedition, it has been calculated that it would have required about 90,000 marks for its continued support (not counting the initial costs of equipment). Most of this sum, which would have been in silver pennies, would have had to be taken with it, imposing a considerable burden to be carried by carts and on baggage animals. As the expedition started, Frederick sent home a number of recruits who were ill-armed or lacking resources or discipline. He wanted his army to be as militarily effective as possible and not to be hampered by a large number of non-combatants, as that of Conrad III had been, 'since a weak and unwarlike crowd was customarily more of a hindrance than a help to such a difficult expedition'.[23]

Frederick had undoubtedly learned from his experience on his uncle's crusade forty years earlier. The expedition which eventually departed in May 1189 was probably about 15,000 strong, with some 3,000 knights. Only a few lay princes took part: his second son Duke Frederick of Swabia, Duke Berthold of Merania and the margraves of Baden and Vohburg. But there were also eight bishops from Germany and two from Burgundy, as well as a Hungarian bishop who subsequently joined them, and no less than 26 counts. In all, the contemporary 'History of the Expedition' named some seventy persons of consequence who took part in the expedition, although this author also named and shamed several prominent figures who had taken the cross and failed to fulfil their vows, including the dukes of Brabant and Limburg and the Bishop of Speyer.[24] Duke Leopold of Austria and Landgrave Ludwig (III) of Thuringia subsequently travelled by sea and joined the crusade in the Holy Land, as did a number of north Germans who left Bremen by ship in April 1189 and sailed via Portugal and through the Straits of Gibraltar, arriving in the east more than a year later.

The early stages went smoothly. The Duke of Austria and King Béla of Hungary welcomed the emperor and furnished ample supplies – the king providing grain, and wagons to carry it, and sheep and cattle, while his queen also presented the emperor with a large tent to use on the campaign, a type of marquee with four rooms. While the army was in Hungary Frederick issued some stringent regulations to maintain discipline – above all to prevent clashes between his troops and the local inhabitants. Problems began when the expedition crossed into what was, at least nominally, Byzantine territory on 1 July 1189. The local governor at Branichevo was superficially friendly. But as the army marched on into the heavily forested region of 'Bulgaria', it faced increasing attacks on stragglers and foragers by men whom the Germans assumed were acting on the orders of the Byzantine authorities. There were also problems about the route – the guides provided by the governor of Branichevo led them astray, which the Germans assumed was done deliberately. The Hungarians who had joined the army led them back to the correct route – the old Byzantine military road through the Balkans. Then envoys from Constantinople arrived who claimed that the emperor there was unaware of the arrival of the western emperor and his army, even though, as Frederick pointed out, he had sent an embassy on ahead to inform the Greek ruler of precisely that. The Germans attributed all these events to a deliberate attempt to delay their march. By contrast, Stephen Nemanja was at pains to provide the army with supplies.

After the army left Nish on 31 July the attacks on the marching columns grew worse and the German response more brutal, with neither side offering quarter. The swords, armour and crossbows of the Germans proved devastatingly effective, while those attackers who were captured were summarily hanged as bandits. When the army arrived at Sofia on 13 August there was no sign of the market that the emperor's envoys had promised, and the road was blocked by fallen trees. Scouts also reported that the passes along the route were held by Greek troops – although this force was probably intended only to shadow the crusade

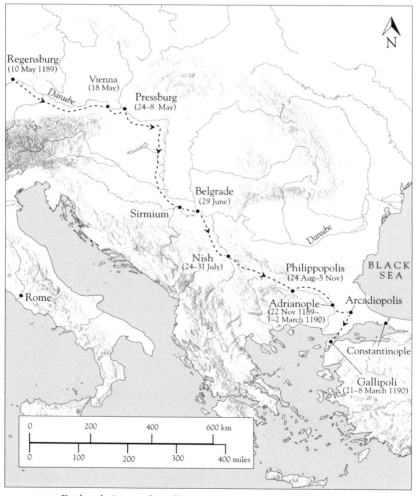

Frederick I's crusade in Europe, 1189–90.

Frederick and his sons Henry and Philip, and Frederick on the march in the Bulgarian forest, illuminations from Peter of Eboli, *Liber ad honorem Augusti*, c. 1195–7.

army. A picked force of five hundred knights was sent on ahead
to force a passage for the rest of the army, which reached
Philippopolis (modern Plovdiv) on 24 August. Whereas the guer-
rilla attacks on the army between Branichevo and Nish were
probably the work of the local populace, acting on their own
initiative, this was the first direct clash with Byzantine troops. At
about the same time news arrived that Frederick's envoys had
been arrested at Constantinople, and then a letter arrived from
Isaac, refusing the army transit. Hardly surprisingly, the worst
possible interpretation was placed on this.

> He did this because he wanted to gain the favour of his
> friend and confederate the Saracen Saladin, the enemy
> of the Cross and of all Christians. The whole army was
> infuriated about this, and thereafter they freely plundered
> the property of the Greeks, and destroyed what they did
> not plunder.[25]

The army remained at Philippopolis for more than two
months, living off the grain stored there and harvesting the vines
and other autumn crops. Detachments were sent out through
Thrace to capture other towns and acquire supplies. Some of the
local inhabitants indeed offered to organize markets for the army
in return for being spared plundering. In early November the army
moved south to Adrianople, a key strategic centre in southern
Thrace and only 210 kilometres (130 mi.) from Constantinople.
But despite the urging of some of his men and promises of assistance from Stephen Nemanja and other Balkan warlords who
had thrown off Byzantine rule, Frederick had no wish to attack
the empire's capital. Rather, he wished to press on to relieve the
Holy Land. His problem was that whereas the Byzantines posed
no real military threat to his formidable army, he needed their
ships to cross the Bosporus onto the Asiatic shore. Furthermore,

since in his eyes the Byzantines had broken their promises to him and were not to be trusted, he was understandably wary of an attack on isolated sections of his troops while that crossing was taking place. During the early autumn he sent a letter back to King Henry in Germany asking him to obtain galleys from the Italian cities to meet his army at the Dardanelles in March, and to forward him more money.[26] But such operations were notoriously hard to coordinate at long range, and there was no guarantee that all the Italian powers would cooperate. (In the event the Pisans, traditional allies of the emperor, did provide some ships, but a Venetian trading convoy coming to Constantinople refused to assist.) In the meanwhile, he allowed his troops to ravage Thrace, both to support the army for what was becoming a lengthy stay, and to intimidate the Byzantine emperor into providing the transport he needed. Isaac Angelos released the German ambassadors in early October, but otherwise little was achieved for the next few months, as envoys criss-crossed between the two sides, and argued about the terms of an agreement that would allow the crossing. Relations were not improved when, right at the beginning of this process, Isaac sent a letter in which he called himself 'Emperor of the Romans', addressed to the 'king of the Germans'.[27]

Isaac might have been wiser to have done everything possible to hurry the Germans on their way, and thus avoid the devastation of a wide swathe of his European territory. If he thought that the German emperor would abandon his enterprise and return home, he had clearly mistaken his man, and he was fortunate that Frederick was genuinely committed to the crusade and had no wish to attack his empire. As it was, it took until February 1190 for a treaty finally to be concluded. In the intervening period the Crusading army seems to have been well supplied: 'overflowing with booty taken from these Greek enemies', although this had an adverse effect on its discipline.[28] Eventually Isaac conceded, agreeing to provide enough ships to transport the entire army, including its horses, to keep his own forces at a distance and his warships in harbour while the crossing was taking place, and to give Frederick 22 high-ranking hostages as sureties that he would observe these terms. He would also ensure that markets would be available on the Asiatic shore.[29] The army left Adrianople in two divisions on 1–2 March; reached Gallipoli, where the crossing was to take place, three weeks later; and after some delay because of heavy rain was ferried across the straits during the week after Easter, on 26–8 March.

Once the army was on the Asiatic shore, it was decided to abandon its carts and wagons, and to carry all the baggage and supplies on pack animals. The Roman roads across Asia Minor were still there, and indeed Frederick's army followed one such, but since the arrival of the Turks more than a century earlier they had probably not been maintained, and in some cases steps had been cut into the steeper sections, which made the use of wheeled transport impossible. This meant, however, that less could be carried, and increased the problem of food supply. For the first month progress through Byzantine territory was reasonably smooth, although there were still skirmishes and attacks on stragglers. Frederick generally restrained his men, and, for example, prevented his advance guard launching a full-scale attack on Philadelphia. Once the expedition passed into Turkish territory at the end of April, harassing attacks immediately commenced. Frederick had hoped that his previous agreements with Sultan Kilij-Arslan would prevent this, and the Germans naturally assumed that the failure to do so was deliberate treachery. In fact, the problem was rather that the sultan's authority was weak; even his sons were becoming increasingly independent and he had little or no control over the nomadic Turcomans in his lands. For three weeks the army marched eastwards, enduring almost daily attacks which were beaten off, but suffering increasingly from

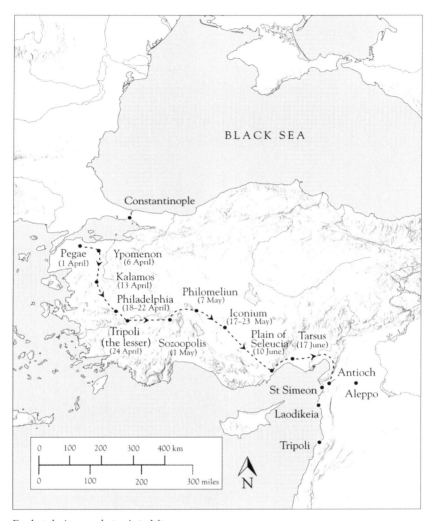

Frederick I's crusade in Asia Minor, 1190.

hunger, 'crueller than any enemy'. The army had already been
short of food when it left Greek territory; by mid-May the troops
were beginning to eat their horses, and the rank and file who
were already on foot suffered most.[30] Frederick nevertheless kept
his army well in hand and avoided a Turkish ambush by an adroit

change of route, guided by a prisoner, and on 17 May they arrived outside the Turkish capital, Iconium (Konya). Negotiations for a truce proved abortive, and the next day the army's advance guard, led by the emperor's son, Duke Frederick of Swabia, stormed the city. The sultan, now besieged in the citadel, agreed to an armistice, to provide a market for supplies and to give hostages. Once replenished, the army left Iconium on 23 May, and despite some skirmishing with the Turcomans – but on nowhere near the same scale as before – reached the border of Cilician Armenia, friendly Christian territory, a week later. The army was still hungry – the market at Iconium had provided only a temporary respite – and some of the leading men were so sick that they had to be carried in litters, but it was no longer under attack, and after traversing a difficult route through the Anti-Taurus mountains, on the morning of 10 June 1190 it debouched onto the fertile plain of Seleucia.

A few hours later the army soon arrived at the river Saleph (now, in Turkish, the Göksu). Accounts of what happened next vary. The emperor decided to ford the river on horseback. He may, as the 'History of the Expedition' described, have been swept away, or knocked from his horse by the force of the river. However, the earliest known source, a newsletter written immediately after the event, possibly by Bishop Gottfried of Würzburg, said that Frederick forded the river successfully, had lunch, but then, because it was a very hot day, decided to cool down by a swim in the river and drowned.[31]

Despite this shattering blow, which was clearly very damaging to the morale of an army much weakened by privation, this was not the end of the expedition. Frederick of Swabia, who had already distinguished himself in the fighting in the Balkans and Asia Minor, took command, and two to three weeks later brought the army, still a cohesive unit, to Antioch, where his father's body was interred in the cathedral. (His intestines had already been removed and buried in the cathedral at Tarsus.) It was soon after that disaster struck, as the army was ravaged by an epidemic, possibly dysentery, as at Rome in 1167. According to the 'History of the Expedition', 'there was such widespread sickness and death there that scarcely anyone was spared, of whatever age, for both noble and poor, young and old were all struck down indiscriminately.'[32] One of the first to die was Bishop Gottfried of Würzburg, on 8 July. Bishop Martin of Meissen died a few days later. Many others followed, either immediately at Antioch, or lingering on weakened to perish later in the year. Four other bishops died, along with the Margrave of Baden and at least eight counts. A few survivors returned home soon afterwards, notably the imperial marshal Henry of Kalden – it is possible that he was summoned by Henry VI, whom he was accompanying in Italy as early as March 1191. Others went with Frederick of Swabia to join the siege of Acre, where the duke died in January 1191, aged only 24. That was really the end of Barbarossa's crusade – most of the Germans who took part in the eventual capture of Acre in July 1191 were those who had come subsequently by sea.

Epilogue

rederick's death while leading what was seen as a divinely sanctioned expedition to recover the Holy Land for Christianity, however anticlimactic the circumstances, might have been seen as the fitting conclusion to a long and heroic life. Although a few of the German commentators embroidered the circumstances of his death to provide a more appropriately religious element – claiming that he confessed or called on God's aid as he was drowning – some were remarkably matter-of-fact about it. One at least, the chronicler of the Saxon monastery of Stederburg, was damning. He claimed that he could say 'nothing glorious and nothing worthy of memory' about the emperor except that he died 'ingloriously' in exile.[1] This jaundiced view may reflect some lingering loyalty felt to Henry the Lion in eastern Saxony. Other chroniclers, writing during the early thirteenth century, knew that Germany had dissolved into civil war after 1198, and were conscious that Frederick's reign had not secured long-term peace, and so were hardly disposed to write encomia about him.

In many ways the crusade had seen Frederick at his best. It was not only one of the largest expeditions but probably the best-prepared such expedition up to this point. He had clearly learned lessons from the failure of King Conrad's expedition in which he had taken part as a young man. He had done his best through diplomacy to secure an uninterrupted passage, even though, as it happened, circumstances were against him. He had maintained discipline and a tight marching order under exceptionally trying circumstances. Even under Turkish attack, his army had marched about 20 kilometres (12½ mi.) a day and had crossed Asia Minor in less than three months (the First Crusade had taken considerably longer). His tactical command had been assured, although he was greatly assisted here by Frederick of Swabia. He had also kept his objective in mind throughout, refusing to become sidetracked into an attack on Constantinople, despite his own army's exasperation with the Byzantines and offers of assistance from the various Balkan enemies of Isaac Angelos. Although by the time of his death his troops were weakened by hunger, and probably already by disease, they were still an army in being, in friendly territory, and receiving supplies from the Armenians. That they did not have more effect on the campaign being fought out in Palestine was due to the epidemic at Antioch, but Saladin had been worried enough by news of Frederick's progress to withdraw troops who were desperately needed at the siege of Acre and send them north to defend against him. Frederick had shown courage, determination, military expertise and considerable diplomatic finesse – as he had in Italy in the 1180s. Here he seems to have learned from previous mistakes.

Yet if we consider his reign overall, it was hardly an unmitigated success. Most obviously, his attempt to reassert effective imperial rule in northern Italy, to which he had devoted much of his time and resources, had failed. The treaty of Konstanz had preserved some remnants of that authority, but the emperor had been forced to concede self-government to the northern cities – even if in central Italy imperial rule was still a reality. Even at the height of the struggle he had only been able to continue his campaigns by exploiting divisions among the cities and relying on his local allies. And after his apparent success in defeating

Milan in 1162, the actions of his officials and the emperor's own insensitivity had alienated not only his former opponents but also most of his allies. The renewal of the campaign against the Lombard League in 1174, which led to the defeat at Legnano, was more a result of stubbornness and a refusal to admit failure than an undertaking with any realistic chance of success.

Much the same could be said about the attempt to dominate the papacy and impose a pro-imperial pope, and the papal schism that this created. How far Frederick's own agents, above all Otto of Wittelsbach and Rainald of Dassel, may have embroiled him in this is a good question, but it seems unlikely that they were operating without taking his wishes into account. It may have seemed in 1160 that there was a reasonable chance that Victor IV might be accepted as the legitimate pope, but if this were so, then the emperor must have been swiftly disillusioned when the rest of Christendom speedily accepted Alexander III. Yet Frederick continued obstinately to persist, not just until Victor's death, which might have been understandable, but for another thirteen years after that. He seems once again to have stubbornly refused to accept that his policy was mistaken and also to have been driven by a personal dislike of Alexander III. Yet the latter was more of a pragmatist, and less extreme, than some of his predecessors. He may, for example, have excommunicated Frederick, but he never sought to declare his rulership invalid or encourage rebellion in Germany against him. The consequences were not just to split Christendom for some seventeen years, or to make the campaigns against the Lombard cities more difficult. The fallout from the schism continued to cause problems for imperial–papal relations into the 1180s, and in the long run to create a lasting suspicion at the papal court, not just against Frederick but against his dynasty. In 1200, when the throne of Germany was in dispute between Frederick's youngest son Philip and Otto, a son of Henry the Lion, Pope Innocent III made his views clear in a secret memorandum to the cardinals, in which he listed a long list of attacks by the Staufer upon the Church, in which the most important of all was Frederick's promotion of the schism. How could the pope support the candidacy of a member of this family against a descendant of Emperor Lothar, who had been a friend and loyal servant of the Church?[2]

One apparently very successful outcome of the reign was the eventual acquisition of the Kingdom of Sicily by Henry VI in 1194 as a result of his marriage to the Sicilian princess Constance eight years earlier – even if this outcome might have seemed unlikely when the marriage took place. This gained the Staufer a wealthy kingdom that was strategically placed to dominate the central Mediterranean. Yet the consequences of this were by no means entirely beneficial. The papacy was henceforth justifiably fearful that the union of the empire and the Kingdom of Sicily would make the emperors even more insistent on their rights in the disputed territories in central Italy and more overbearing in their relations with the Apostolic See. This issue persisted throughout the reign of Barbarossa's grandson Frederick II and ultimately sabotaged his rule. Furthermore, if Barbarossa's Italian campaigns had made him a semi-absentee ruler of Germany for much of his reign, possession of the Kingdom of Sicily encouraged this tendency even more. Frederick II, who had been born in Italy and brought up in Sicily, spent very little time in Germany. After his imperial coronation in 1220 he spent only thirteen months of the last thirty years of his rule north of the Alps. In his absence princely rule in Germany was consolidated even further.

Yet this was hardly a new development, and the reign of Frederick Barbarossa marked a crucial, and probably irrevocable, stage in this process. Frederick admittedly, and seemingly without opposition, ensured the succession of his eldest surviving son as king. Henry VI tried to go further and in 1196 attempted to

Henry VI as king of Sicily, illumination from Peter of Eboli, *Liber ad honorem Augusti, c.* 1195–7.

persuade the princes to acknowledge the Staufer as the *de jure* as well as *de facto* hereditary monarchs of Germany but was unable to do so. They did, admittedly, agree to elect his infant son as king, but when Henry died unexpectedly in September 1197, at the age of only 31, the rights of the absentee child were disregarded and a disputed election led to civil war. The tension between the elective and hereditary principles was still not entirely resolved, but the balance tipped heavily in favour of the former. The issue of German rulership was, however, much more one of structure than of personalities, or of hereditary versus elective kingship. Frederick I's rule in Germany was based on three things. First, there was the great wealth of the Staufer, which Frederick managed to reunite in his own hands, and considerably increase during the course of the reign. Combined with the Crown lands, this meant that he was by a long way the greatest and most powerful territorial lord in the Reich. Second, he was, as we have seen, still very much in control of the Church in Germany, and the leaders of that Church were, with rare exceptions, obedient to his rule – even if, as in the later stages of the schism, many of them were by no means happy with his policy. Third, there was the prestige of the kingship and of the imperial office, and the view of the princes that the emperor was *their* representative and that his prestige mattered to them. This was clearly shown during the near riot against the papal legates at the diet of Besançon in 1157. Frederick's success in keeping the peace among the princes, and his very longevity, enhanced this. In many ways the great assembly at Mainz in 1184 was the high point of his reign, certainly in Germany, where the emperor displayed himself as the great ruler among his princes and other nobles. The suggestion that by taking part in the chivalric, and non-violent, tournament there the emperor therefore was admitting that he was only first among equals, and not the ruler chosen by God, seems to be wide of the mark. On great occasions Frederick was still a prestigious and even charismatic monarch, although assemblies on the scale of 1184, and in 1188 to promote the crusade, were unusual.

But at a time when the kings of England and Sicily, followed soon afterwards and to a lesser extent by the king of France, were creating administrative and legal structures for their whole kingdom, this was precisely what was not happening in Germany. Such structures were being created, but in the nascent principalities, not for the kingdom as a whole. Whereas, for example, in England and Sicily the coinage was a royal monopoly, in Germany the ruler was only one among many who possessed mints. The number of such mints greatly increased as the economy of Germany expanded during the twelfth century. Yet when Barbarossa died in 1190 only 26 out of more than 200 mints there belonged to the king, about 80 to lay lords, and the rest to churches. While private warfare was forbidden in other kingdoms, in Germany the royal land peace edicts did not seek to ban warfare, but only to control it and to mitigate its malign effects. And although Frederick was able to bring about the downfall of Henry the Lion, those who profited directly from this were the princes, and Henry's enemies appear to have pushed the emperor into punishing Henry more than he really intended. Furthermore, as the reign went on Frederick's itinerary in Germany became more constricted, and fewer of the great men of the realm regularly attended his court. Thus the range of personal kingship diminished.

In the end, the foundations of Frederick's imperial authority proved to be built on sand. Direct rule in northern Italy proved impossible to enforce and imperial rule over central Italy collapsed after the death of Henry VI. The civil war after 1198 began the erosion of the landed power of the Staufer in Germany, which was greatly increased during the last years of Frederick II when the absentee emperor was at war with the papacy. During

the civil war the rival kings were forced to surrender much of
their power over the Church, although largely to the profit of
the various princely and some comital dynasties, who came more
and more to control their local bishoprics. The prestige of the
imperial office slowly diminished, and the rulers after Frederick
II, few of whom ever received imperial coronation, became more
and more first among equals – and sometimes not even that. The
future in Germany lay with the princes; and while the development of their authority was slow and evolutionary, the reign of
Frederick Barbarossa – supposedly the high point of German
monarchy – marked a vital stage in that process.

REFERENCES

Abbreviations

Arnold of Lübeck   *The Chronicle of Arnold of Lübeck*, trans. G. A. Loud (Crusade Texts in Translation 33) (London, 2019)

Boso   *Boso's Life of Alexander III*, trans. G. M. Ellis (Oxford, 1973)

Briefbuch Abt Wibalds   *Das Briefbuch Abt Wibalds von Stablo und Corvey*, ed. Martina Hartmann, with Heinz Zatschek and Timothy Reuter (3 vols, MGH Briefe der deutschen Kaiserzeit, Hanover, 2012)

Crusade of FB   *The Crusade of Frederick Barbarossa: The History of the Expedition of the Emperor Frederick and Related Texts*, trans. G. A. Loud (Crusade Texts in Translation 19) (Farnham, 2010)

Dipl. Fred. 1   *Die Urkunden Friedrichs 1*, ed. Heinrich Appelt (5 vols, MGH Diplomatum Regum et Imperatorum Germaniae, 10, Hanover, 1975–90)

GF   *The Deeds of Frederick Barbarossa by Otto of Freising and His Continuator, Rahewin*, trans. Charles Christopher Mierow (New York, 1953) [abbreviation = *Gesta Frederici*]

GF in Lombardia   *Gesta Federici 1. Imperatoris in Lombardia auctore cive Mediolanensi (Annales Mediolanenses Maiores)*, ed. Oswald Holder-Egger (MGH SRG, Hanover, 1892)

Helmold   *The Chronicle of the Slavs by Helmold, Priest of Bosau*, trans. Francis J. Tschan (New York, 1935)

Historia Welforum   *Historia Welforum Weingartensis*, ed. Ludwig Weiland, MGH SS xxi.454–72.

MGH   Monumenta Germaniae Historica, following the usual abbreviations for subseries (SS = Scriptores, SRG = Scriptores Rerum Germanicarum, etc.)

| *Otto Morena* | *Das Geschichtswerk des Otto Morena und seiner Fortsetzer*, ed. Ferdinand Güterbock (MGH SRG, Berlin, 1930) |
| *Otto von St. Blasien* | *Die Chronik von Otto von St. Blasien und die Marbacher Annalen*, ed. Franz-Josef Schmale (Darmstadt, 1998) |

Introduction

1 The king of Germany had since 962 been accustomed to being crowned in Rome by the pope as 'Roman emperor', but until he received this imperial coronation he remained only king. Thus Frederick Barbarossa was crowned king of Germany at Aachen in March 1152 but was only crowned emperor in June 1155. After 1273 only a minority of German kings were crowned emperor.

2 Aenio Silvio Piccolomini (Pius II), quoted by Peter H. Wilson, *The Holy Roman Empire: A Thousand Years of Europe's History* (London, 2016), p. 278.

3 *GF*, book III, ch. 8, p. 180.

4 *Carmen de Gestis Frederici I in Lombardia*, ed. Irene Schmale-Ott (MGH SRG, Hanover, 1965), p. xxviii.

5 Karl Hampe, *Germany under the Salian and Hohenstaufen Emperors*, trans. Ralph Bennett (Oxford, 1973), pp. 153–4. This English translation was made from the twelfth German edition of 1968, edited by Hampe's pupil Friedrich Baethgen.

6 No contemporary source mentions Alberto, whose name first appeared in the late fourteenth-century chronicle of Galvano Fiamma and was probably invented by him.

7 Karl Leyser, 'Frederick Barbarossa: Court and Country', in Leyser, *Communications and Power in Medieval Europe: The Gregorian Revolution and Beyond*, ed. Timothy Reuter (London, 1994), p. 143.

8 Karl Marx, *Der achtzehnte Brumaire des Louis Bonaparte*, 2nd edn (Hamburg, 1869), p. 1 (English translation by Benjamin Pohl).

1 Context

1 *Widukind of Corvey, Deeds of the Saxons*, trans. B. S. and D. S. Bachrach (Washington, DC, 2014), III.49, p. 129.

2 *GF*, II.30, p. 147.

3 *Die Urkunden Heinrichs ii und Arduins*, ed. Harry Bresslau, Hermann Bloch and Robert Holtzmann (MGH Diplomata Regum et Imperatorum Germaniae 3, Hanover, 1900–1903), pp. 326–7 no. 277.

4 *Die Urkunden Konrads ii*, ed. Harry Bresslau (MGH Diplomata Regum et Imperatorum Germaniae 4, Hanover, 1909), p. 263 no. 198.

5 *Dipl. Fred. i*, ii.432 no. 502. Whether the initiative in the canonization came from the emperor himself or from the canons of Aachen is a matter of some debate.

6 *The Play of Antichrist*, trans. John Wright (Toronto, 1967), pp. 70, 74–5.

7 Matthew 16:18. This sentence works better in Latin, where there is a wordplay between *Petrus* (Peter) and *petra* (a rock).

8 *GF*, I.12, p. 45.

9 *Historia Welforum*, ch. 13, p. 462.

10 The counts palatine (German *Pfalzgraf*) – there was only one for each historic duchy – were effectively independent of ducal control and held their office/rank directly from the emperor. They were classed among the imperial princes.

11 *Chronicles of the Investiture Contest: Frutolf of Michelsberg and His Continuators*, trans. T.J.H. McCarthy (Manchester, 2014), p. 278.

2 Early Years, 1152–8

1 *GF*, II.1, p. 115.

2 Ibid., I.70, p. 111; II.2, p. 116.

3 *Briefbuch Abt Wibalds*, iii.814–16 no. 386.

4 *Gilbert of Mons, Chronicle of Hainaut*, trans. Laura Napran (Woodbridge, 2005), pp. 54–5.

5 *Otto Morena*, p. 167.

6 *GF*, IV.86, p. 331.

7 *Dipl. Fred. i*, i.39–44 no. 25.

8 *Otto von St. Blasien*, p. 32.

9 Or possibly, 'as God is my witness'.

10 *Briefbuch Abt Wibalds*, iii.824–6 no. 393.

11 Ibid., iii.800–809 nos 382–3.

12 *Dipl. Fred. i*, i.183–4 no. 108.

13 *GF*, II.28, pp. 142–4.

14 *Helmold*, I.81, p. 214.

15 *Dipl. Fred. i*, i.183–4 no. 108; *GF*, II.39, p. 155.

16 *GF*, II.43, p. 160.

17 Ibid., II.46, p. 163.
18 *Dipl. Fred. I*, i.179–81 no. 106.
19 Ibid., i.259–60 no. 151.
20 *GF*, II.47, p. 165.
21 Ibid., III.6–7, pp. 178–80.
22 *Dipl. Fred. I*, i.335–7 no. 201.
23 *The Play of Antichrist*, trans. John Wright (Toronto, 1967), pp. 73, 75–6. Cf. above, p. 22.
24 First Epistle of Peter 2:17.
25 For the texts of all these letters, *GF*, III.8–11, 16–17, pp. 180–86, 190–94.

3 Italy, 1158–78

1 *GF*, II.13, p. 128.
2 *Die Tafelgüterverzeichnis des römischen Königs (Ms. Bonn S. 1559)*, ed. Carlrichard Brühl and Theo Kölzer (Cologne, 1979), pp. 27–8, 53.
3 *GF in Lombardia*, p. 30.
4 *GF*, IV.1–10, pp. 232–43, especially 238, 242.
5 *Dipl. Fred. I*, ii.42–4 no. 246 (3 December 1158).
6 *GF in Lombardia*, pp. 35–6.
7 *Otto Morena*, pp. 63–6.
8 His predecessor, Archbishop Frederick (II), had died at Pavia in December 1158.
9 The best account, probably by an eyewitness, comes in Vincent of Prague, *Annales*, ed. Wilhelm Wattenbach, MGH ss xvii.678–9.
10 *Dipl. Fred. I*, ii.152–3 no. 326.
11 *Otto Morena*, pp. 158–9.
12 Ibid., p. 166.
13 Ibid., pp. 172–3.
14 *Boso*, p. 64; *Otto Morena*, p. 176.
15 *Boso*, p. 59.
16 *Quellen zur deutschen Verfassungs-, Wirtschafts- und Sozialgeschichte bis 1250*, ed. L. Weinrich (Darmstadt, 1977), pp. 266–78 no. 70.
17 *Otto Morena*, pp. 180–81. After the death of his son, who had taken over his *History*, Otto once again took up his pen and wrote a continuation describing Barbarossa's 1166–8 expedition.
18 Ibid., p. 209.
19 *Otto von St. Blasien*, pp. 60–62.
20 *Dipl. Fred. I*, ii.481–2 no. 535.
21 *GF in Lombardia*, p. 62.

22 *Boso*, p. 88.

23 Ibid., p. 91.

24 *Dipl. Fred. I*, iii.149–52 no. 648: the witness list is also important evidence for the reinforcements Frederick had received.

25 *Boso*, p. 98.

26 *Dipl. Fred. I*, iii.154–5 no. 650.

27 Ibid., iii.161–5 no. 658.

28 *Die Tegernseer Briefsammlung des 12. Jahrhunderts*, ed. Helmut Plechl (MGH Briefe der deutscher Kaiserzeit 8, Hanover, 2002), pp. 43–4 no. 29.

29 *Otto von St. Blasien*, p. 72.

30 *Priester Konrad, Chronik des Lauterberg (Petersburg bei Halle/S)*, ed. Klaus Naß (MGH, SRG, Wiesbaden, 2020), p. 144.

31 The most detailed account of the conference and of the diplomacy that preceded it was written by the Archbishop of Salerno, the head of the Sicilian delegation, *Romualdi Salernitani Chronicon*, ed. C. A. Garufi (Rerum Italicarum Scriptores, Città di Castello, 1935), pp. 269–94.

32 *Urkundenbuch des Hochstift Halberstadt und seiner Bischöfe 1 bis 1236*, ed. Gustav Schmidt (Leipzig, 1883), 231–2 no. 268; *Dipl. Fred. I*, iii.146–7 no. 645, 153–4 no. 649; *Mainzer Urkundenbuch*, vol. II: *Die Urkunden seit dem Tode Erzbischof Adelberts I. (1137) bis zum Tode Erzbischof Konrads (1200)*, part II: *1176–1200*, ed. Peter Acht (Darmstadt, 1971), 876–85 no. 531.

4 Germany, 1158–78

1 *Historia Welforum*, pp. 469–70 ch. 30–31; *Otto von St. Blasien*, pp. 50–52.

2 *Chronica Regia Coloniensis*, ed. Georg Waitz (MGH SRG, Hanover, 1880), pp. 115–16; *Dipl. Fred. I*, ii.423–6 no. 497, 445–6 no. 511.

3 *Helmold*, p. 265.

4 *Die Admonter Briefsammlung nebst ergänzenden Briefe*, ed. Günther Hödl and Peter Classen (MGH Briefe der deutschen Kaiserzeit 6, Munich, 1983), pp. 193–6 no. 33, at p. 195.

5 *Dipl. Fred. I*, i.132–4 no. 80, 332–3 no. 199.

6 Ibid., iii.112–13 no. 620.

7 Ibid., ii.481–2 no. 535.

8 Ibid., ii.486–8 nos 539–40.

9 *Gesta Treverorum*, ed. Georg Waitz, MGH SS xxiv.382.

10 *GF*, IV.82, pp. 329–30.

11 *Dipl. Fred. I*, iii.35–6 no. 566. Frederick's eldest son had died in
    1168/9, and his third son, originally called Conrad, was then
    rechristened Frederick.

12 Ibid., iii.119–20 no. 625.

13 *Historia Welforum, Continuatio Staingademensis*, p. 472.

14 *Otto von St. Blasien*, p. 62.

15 Ibid., p. 64.

16 *Dipl. Fred. I*, iii.42–3 no. 571 (July 1170).

17 He had been born at Nijmegen in November 1165.

18 Above, p. 68.

19 *Dipl. Fred. I*, ii.412–14 no. 491, at p. 411.

20 *Arnold of Lübeck*, III.9, p. 108.

21 *Dipl. Fred. I*, iii.328–30 no. 774.

22 Ibid., iii.310–11 no. 757.

23 Ibid., iii.123–4 no. 629.

24 Ibid., iii.5–7 no. 546.

5 The Last Years, 1178–90

1 *Arnold of Lübeck*, I.4, 9, pp. 46, 51–3.

2 Ibid., II.1–2, 10, pp. 63–5, 73 (quote p. 65).

3 *Otto von St. Blasien*, p. 70.

4 *Chronica Regia Coloniensis*, ed. Georg Waitz (MGH SRG, Hanover,
    1880), p. 130.

5 *Dipl. Fred. I*, ii.362–3 no. 795.

6 *Die Jüngere Hildesheimer Briefsammlung*, ed. Rolf de Kegel (MGH
    Briefe der deutschen Kaiserzeit 7, Hanover, 1995), pp. 102–3 no. 55.

7 *Arnold of Lübeck*, II.22, p. 91.

8 *Gilbert of Mons, Chronicle of Hainaut*, trans. Laura Napran
    (Woodbridge, 2005), p. 89.

9 *Arnold of Lübeck*, III.9, p. 108.

10 *Chronicle of Hainaut*, p. 88.

11 *Dipl. Fred. I*, iv.68–77 no. 848.

12 Ibid., iv.147–51 no. 896.

13 The fullest account is by *Arnold of Lübeck*, III.9, pp. 108–11.

14 Ibid., III.12, pp. 117–19.

15 MGH *Constitutiones et Acta Publica*, 1 (911–1197), ed. Ludwig
    Weiland (Hanover, 1893), 444–8 nos 315–16.

16 *Otto von St. Blasien*, p. 174.

17 'The History of the Expedition of the Emperor Frederick', in
    Crusade of FB, p. 43.

18 *Chronica Regia Coloniensis*, p. 139.

19 *Arnold of Lübeck*, IV.7, p. 147.

20 *Crusade of* FB, pp. 209–12.

21 The best contemporary account is *Gesta Treverorum, Continuatio Tertia*, ed. Georg Waitz, MGH SS XXIV.388–9.

22 *Crusade of* FB, p. 46 (quoting Matthew 10:16).

23 'History of the Pilgrims', in *Crusade of* FB, p. 144.

24 'History of the Expedition of the Emperor Frederick', in *Crusade of* FB, pp. 47–56.

25 Ibid., p. 69.

26 Ibid., pp. 70–72.

27 Ibid., p. 78.

28 Ibid., p. 86.

29 Ibid., pp. 90–92.

30 Ibid., p. 104.

31 Ibid., pp. 115–16, 172.

32 Ibid., p. 117.

Epilogue

1 *Annales Stederbergenses*, MGH SS XVI.223.

2 *Regestum Innocentii III Papae super Negotio Romani Imperii*, ed. Friedrich Kempf (Rome, 1947), pp. 75–91 no. 29.

FURTHER READING

Select Bibliography of Works in English

Arnold, Benjamin, *German Knighthood, 1050–1300* (Oxford, 1985)
—, *Medieval Germany, 500–1300: A Political Interpretation*
    (Basingstoke, 1997)
—, *Princes and Territories in Medieval Germany* (Cambridge, 1991)
Bolton, Brenda, and Anne J. Duggan, eds, *Adrian IV, the English
    Pope (1154–1159): Studies and Texts* (Aldershot, 2003)
Clarke, Peter D., and Anne J. Duggan, eds, *Pope Alexander III:
    The Art of Survival* (Aldershot, 2012)
Freed, John B., *Frederick Barbarossa: The Prince and the Myth*
    (New Haven, CT, 2016)
Jordan, Karl, *Henry the Lion: A Biography*, trans. P. S. Falla
    (Oxford, 1986)
Leerssen, Joep, 'Once upon a Time in Germany: Medievalism,
    Academic Romanticism and Nationalism', in *The Making
    of Medieval History*, ed. G. A. Loud and Martial Staub
    (Woodbridge, 2017), pp. 101–26
Leyser, Karl, 'Frederick Barbarossa and the Hohenstaufen
    Polity' and 'Frederick Barbarossa: Court and Country', in Leyser,
    *Communications and Power in Medieval Europe: The Gregorian
    Revolution and Beyond*, ed. Timothy Reuter (London, 1994),
    pp. 115–55
Loud, G. A., and Jochen Schenk, eds, *The Origins of the German
    Principalities, 1100–1350: Essays by German Historians*
    (London, 2017)
Murray, Alan V., 'Finance and Logistics of the Crusade of Frederick
    Barbarossa', in *In Laudem Hierosolymitani: Studies in Crusades and
    Material Culture in Honour of Benjamin Z. Kedar*, ed. Iris Shagrir,
    Ronnie Ellenblum and Jonathan Riley-Smith (Aldershot, 2007),
    pp. 357–68
Plassmann, Alheydis, 'The King and His Sons: Henry II's and Frederick
    Barbarossa's Succession Strategies Compared', in *Anglo-Norman
    Studies 36, Proceedings of the Battle Conference 2013*, ed. David
    Bates (Woodbridge, 2014), pp. 149–66

—, and Dominik Büschen, eds, *Staufen and Plantagenets: Two Empires in Comparison* (Bonn, 2018)

Raccagni, Gianluca, *The Lombard League, 1167–1225* (Oxford, 2010)

Reuter, Timothy, 'The Medieval German *Sonderweg?* The Empire and Its Rulers in the High Middle Ages' and 'Mandate, Privilege, Court Judgement: Techniques of Rulership in the Age of Frederick Barbarossa', in Reuter, *Medieval Polities and Modern Mentalities*, ed. Janet L. Nelson (Cambridge, 2006), pp. 388–431

Wickham, Chris, *Sleepwalking into a New World: The Emergence of the Italian City Communes in the Twelfth Century* (Princeton, NJ, and Oxford, 2015)

Primary Sources Available in English Translation

Boso's Life of Alexander III, trans. G. M. Ellis (Oxford, 1973)

The Chronicle of Arnold of Lübeck, trans. G. A. Loud (Crusade Texts in Translation 33) (London, 2019)

The Crusade of Frederick Barbarossa: The History of the Expedition of the Emperor Frederick and Related Texts, trans. G. A. Loud (Crusade Texts in Translation 19) (Farnham, 2010)

The Deeds of Frederick Barbarossa by Otto of Freising and His Continuator, Rahewin, trans. Charles Christopher Mierow (New York, 1953)

Gilbert of Mons, Chronicle of Hainaut, trans. Laura Napran (Woodbridge, 2005)

Helmold of Bosau, Chronicle of the Slavs, trans. Francis J. Tschan (New York, 1935)

One should note that several of the key sources for the reign have never been translated into English, notably the chronicles of Otto and Acerbo Morena, Vincent of Prague, Otto of St Blasien, the so-called Royal Chronicle of Cologne and the 'History of the Welfs of Weingarten'. An unpublished partial translation of this last text can, however, be found at https://eprints. whiterose.ac.uk/212783.

Works in Languages Other Than English

This is an even more select list of works that have proved useful while researching and writing this book.

Assmann, Erwin, 'Friedrich Barbarossa Kinder', *Deutsches Archiv für Erforschung des Mittelalters*, XXXIII (1977), pp. 435–72

Ehlers, Joachim, *Heinrich der Löwe: Eine Biographie* (Munich, 2008)

Eickhoff, Ekkehard, *Friedrich Barbarossa im Orient: Kreuzzug und Tod Friedrichs I* (Tübingen, 1977)

Görich, Knut, *Friedrich Barbarossa: Der Erste Stauferkaiser* (Munich, 2022)

—, *Friedrich Barbarossa: Eine Biographie* (Munich, 2011)

—, 'Kanonisation al Mittel der Politik? Der heilige Karl und Friedrich Barbarossa', in *Karlsbilder in Kunst, Literatur und Wissenschaft*, ed. Franz Fuchs and Dorothea Klein (Würzburg, 2015), pp. 95–114

Haverkamp, Alfred, ed., *Friedrich Barbarossa: Handlungsspielräume und Wirkungsweisen des staufischen Kaisers* (Vorträge und Forschungen 40, Sigmaringen, 1992)

Herde, Peter, 'La catastrofe alle porte di Roma dell'agosto 1167: Uno studio storico-epidemiologico', *Bullettino del istituto storico italiano per il medio evo*, XCVI (1990), pp. 175–200

Kölzer, Theo, 'Friedrich Barbarossa und die Reichsfürsten', in *Deutscher Königshof, Hoftag und Reichstag im späteren Mittelalter*, ed. Peter Moraw (Stuttgart, 2002), pp. 3–47

Manselli, Raoul, and Josef Riedmann, eds, *Federico Barbarossa nel dibattito storiografico in Italia e in Germania* (Bologna, 1982)

Opll, Ferdinand, *Das Itinerar Kaiser Friedrich Barbarossas (1152–1190)* (Vienna, 1978)

Plassmann, Alheydis, *Die Struktur des Hofes unter Friedrich I. Barbarossa nach den deutschen Zeugen seiner Urkunden* (Hanover, 1998)

Schlesinger, Walter, 'Bischofssitze, Pfalzen und Städte im deutschen Itinerar Friedrich Barbarossas', in *Ausgewählte Aufsätze von Walter Schlesinger, 1965–1979*, ed. Hans Patze and Fred Schwinde (Vorträge und Forschungen 34, Sigmaringen, 1987), pp. 347–401

Wieczorek, Alfried, Berndt Schneidmüller and Stefan Weinfurter, eds, *Die Staufer und Italien: Drei Innovationsregionen im mittelalterlichen Europa*, 2 vols (Mannheim and Darmstadt, 2010)

ACKNOWLEDGEMENTS

It is a great pleasure to thank both the medievalist colleagues who have read drafts of this book – Prof. Knut Görich (Munich), Prof. Alan Murray (Leeds) and Prof. Benjamin Pohl (Bristol) – and also the friends who have volunteered to read this on behalf of the general reader: Nick and Patricia Beeching and Simeon Underwood. Their comments have all been very helpful. I should also thank Dr Diane Milburn, with whom I visited several Barbarossa-related sites in Saxony and Thuringia almost thirty years ago. Above all, I am grateful to my wife Kate Fenton, not just for her love and support – and superior IT skills, as always – but for drawing the maps and genealogical charts. This book is dedicated to her, and to the memory of a fine German scholar of Frederick Barbarossa whom I knew, and who died recently and far too young.

PHOTO ACKNOWLEDGEMENTS

The author and publishers wish to express their thanks to the sources listed below for illustrative material and/or permission to reproduce it. Some locations of artworks are also given below, in the interest of brevity:

AdobeStock: pp. 82 (Luca), 120 (Sina Ettmer), 138 (modernmovie); Associated Press/Eckehard Schulz/Alamy Stock Photo: p. 111; Biblioteca Apostolica Vaticana, Vatican City (Cod. Vat. Lat. 2001, fol. 1r): p. 160; Bibliothèque nationale de France, Paris (MS Latin 5411, fol. 253r): p. 55; Burgerbibliothek, Bern (Cod. 120.II): pp. 167 (fol. 143r), 178 (fol. 146r); Kate Fenton: pp. 16, 28 (adapted by kind permission of the author from Knut Görich, *Friedrich Barbarossa: Eine Biographie* (Munich, 2011)), 45, 66, 125, 136, 146, 166, 171; Herzog August Bibliothek, Wolfenbüttel (Cod. Guelf. 105 Noviss. 2°, fol. 171v), photo © HAB Wolfenbüttel (CC BY-SA 4.0): p. 139; Hochschul- und Landesbibliothek Fulda (Cod. 100 D 11, fol. 14r): p. 149; Wikimedia Commons: pp. 6 (photo Tilman2007, CC BY-SA 4.0), 11 (photo Clemensfranz, CC BY-SA 4.0), 42 (Stiftskirche St Johannes Evangelist, Selm-Cappenberg, photo Rainer Halama, CC BY-SA 4.0).

INDEX

Page numbers in *italics* refer to illustrations